Complexity and Contradiction in Architecture

Robert Venturi

with an introduction by Vincent Scully

The Museum of Modern Art Papers on Architecture

The Museum of Modern Art, New York
in association with
the Graham Foundation for Advanced Studies in
the Fine Arts, Chicago
Distributed by New York Graphic Society Books/
Little, Brown and Company, Boston

Copyright © The Museum of Modern Art, 1966, 1977
All rights reserved
Second edition 1977, reprinted 1979, 1981, 1983, 1985, 1988
Library of Congress Catalog Card Number 77-77289
Paperbound ISBN 0-87070-282-3
Clothbound ISBN 0-87070-281-5
Second edition designed by Steven Schoenfelder
Printed by Baronet Litho, Inc., Johnstown, New York
Bound by Sendor Bindery, Inc., New York, New York
The Museum of Modern Art
11 West 53 Street
New York, New York 10019
Printed in the United States of America

To the memory of my mother and my father.

Acknowledgments

Most of this book was written in 1962 under a grant from the Graham Foundation. I am also indebted to the American Academy in Rome for the Fellowship, ten years ago, which enabled me to live in Italy.

The following people helped me: Vincent Scully, through his crucial appreciation and criticism when I really needed them; Marian Scully, through her skill, patience and understanding in making the text clearer; Philip Finkelpearl, through his talking with me over the years; Denise Scott Brown, by sharing her insights into architecture and city planning; Robert Stern, through concrete enrichments to the argument; Mrs. Henry Ottmann and Miss Ellen Marsh of the staff of The Museum of Modern Art, through their cooperation in collecting illustrations.

R.V.

Contents

Acknowledgments 6

Foreword 8

Introduction 9

Preface 13

1. Nonstraightforward Architecture:
   A Gentle Manifesto 16

2. Complexity and Contradiction vs.
   Simplification or Picturesqueness 16

3. Ambiguity 20

4. Contradictory Levels:
   The Phenomenon of "Both-And" in Architecture 23

5. Contradictory Levels Continued:
   The Double-Functioning Element 34

6. Accommodation and the Limitations of Order:
   The Conventional Element 41

7. Contradiction Adapted 45

8. Contradiction Juxtaposed 56

9. The Inside and the Outside 70

10. The Obligation Toward the Difficult Whole 88

11. Works 106

Notes 132

Photograph Credits 133

This remarkable study is the first in a series of occasional papers concerned with the theoretical background of modern architecture. Unlike other Museum publications in architecture and design, the series will be independent of the Museum's exhibition program. It will explore ideas too complex for presentation in exhibition form, and authors will represent no single professional group.

Mr. Venturi's book is published by the Museum in collaboration with the Graham Foundation for Advanced Studies in the Fine Arts. It is a particularly appropriate volume with which to inaugurate the series, as the author was originally enabled to work on the text through the aid of a Graham Foundation grant.

Like his buildings, Venturi's book opposes what many would consider Establishment, or at least established, opinions. He speaks with uncommon candor, addressing himself to actual conditions: the ambiguous and sometimes unattractive "facts" in which architects find themselves enmeshed at each moment, and whose confusing nature Venturi would seek to make the basis of architectural design. It is an alternative point of view vigorously championed by Vincent Scully of Yale University, whose introduction contrasts the frustrations of abstractly preconceived architectural order with Venturi's delight in reality—especially in those recalcitrant aspects most architects would seek to suppress or disguise. Venturi's recommendations can be tested immediately: they need not wait on legislation or technology. Problems in the architecture he seeks to supplant are so far from being resolved that, whether or not we agree with his results, we are impelled to grant him an attentive hearing.

Arthur Drexler
Director
Department of Architecture and Design

This is not an easy book. It requires professional commitment and close visual attention, and is not for those architects who, lest they offend them, pluck out their eyes. Indeed, its argument unfolds like a curtain slowly lifting from the eyes. Piece by piece, in close focus after focus, the whole emerges. And that whole is new—hard to see, hard to write about, graceless and inarticulate as only the new can be.

It is a very American book, rigorously pluralistic and phenomenological in its method; one is reminded of Dreiser, laboriously trodding out the way. Yet it is probably the most important writing on the making of architecture since Le Corbusier's *Vers une Architecture,* of 1923. Indeed, at first sight, Venturi's position seems exactly the opposite of Le Corbusier's, its first and natural complement across time.* This is not to say that Venturi is Le Corbusier's equal in persuasiveness or achievement—or will necessarily ever be. Few will attain to that level again. The experience of Le Corbusier's buildings themselves has surely had not a little to do with forming Venturi's ideas. Yet his views do in fact balance those of Le Corbusier as they were expressed in his early writings and as they have generally affected two architectural generations since that time. The older book demanded a noble purism in architecture, in single buildings and in the city as a whole; the new book welcomes the contradictions and complexities of urban experience at all scales. It marks, in this way, a complete shift of emphasis and will annoy some of those who profess to follow Le Corbusier now, exactly as Le Corbusier infuriated many who belonged to the Beaux-Arts then. Hence the books do in fact complement each other; and in one fundamental way they are much the same. Both are by architects who have really learned something from the architecture of the past. Few contemporary architects have been able to do this and have instead tended to take refuge in various systems of what can only be called historical propaganda. For Le Corbusier and Venturi, the experience was personal and direct. Each was thus able to free himself from the fixed patterns of thought and the fashions of his contemporaries, so carrying out Camus' injunction to leave behind for a while "our age and its adolescent furies."

Each learned most from very different things. Le Corbusier's great teacher was the Greek temple, with its isolated body white and free in the landscape, its luminous austerities clear in the sun. In his early polemics he would have his buildings and his cities just that way, and his mature architecture itself came more and more to embody the Greek temple's sculptural, actively heroic character. Venturi's primary inspiration would seem to have come from the Greek temple's historical and archetypal opposite, the urban façades of Italy, with their endless adjustments to the counter-requirements of inside and outside and their inflection with all the business of everyday life: not primarily sculptural actors in vast landscapes but complex spatial containers and definers of streets and squares. Such "accommodation" also becomes a general urban principle for Venturi. In this he again resembles Le Corbusier, in so far as they are both profoundly visual, plastic artists whose close focus upon individual buildings brings with it a new visual and symbolic attitude toward urbanism in general—not the schematic or two-dimensionally diagrammatic view toward which many planners tend, but a set of solid images, architecture itself at its full scale.

Yet again, the images of Le Corbusier and Venturi are diametrically opposed in this regard. Le Corbusier, exercising that side of his many-sided nature which professed Cartesian rigor, generalized in *Vers une Architecture* much more easily than Venturi does here, and presented a clear, general scheme for the whole. Venturi is more fragmentary, moving step by step through more compromised relationships. His conclusions are general only by implication. Yet it seems to me that his proposals, in their recognition of complexity and their respect for what exists, create the most necessary antidote to that cataclysmic purism of contemporary urban renewal which has presently brought so many cities to the brink of catastrophe, and in which Le Corbusier's ideas have now found terrifying vulgarization. They are a hero's dreams applied en masse—as if an

---

* Here I do not forget Bruno Zevi's *Towards an Organic Architecture,* of 1950, which was consciously written as a reply to Le Corbusier. One cannot, however, regard it as a complement to the other or as an advance upon it, since it was hardly more than a reaction against it in favor of "organic" principles which had been formulated by architects other than Zevi and had indeed passed their peak of vitality long before. They had found their best embodiment in the work of Frank Lloyd Wright before 1914 and their clearest verbal statement in his writings of that period.

Achilles were to become the king. That is why, one supposes, Venturi is so consistently anti-heroic, compulsively qualifying his recommendations with an implied irony at every turn. Le Corbusier used irony too, but his was as sharp as a steel-toothed smile. Venturi shrugs his shoulders ruefully and moves on. It is this generation's answer to grandiose pretensions which have shown themselves in practice to be destructive or overblown.

Like all original architects, Venturi makes us see the past anew. He has made me, for example, who once focused upon the proto-Wrightian continuities of the Shingle Style, revalue their equally obvious opposite: the complicated accommodations of inside and outside with which those architects themselves were surely entranced. And he has even called attention once more to the principle of accommodation in Le Corbusier's early plans. So all inventive architects bring their dead to life again as a matter of course. It is appropriate that Le Corbusier and Venturi should come together on the question of Michelangelo, in whose work heroic action and complex qualification found special union. Venturi fixes less than Le Corbusier upon the unified assertion of Michelangelo's conception in St. Peter's but, like Le Corbusier, he sees and, as the fenestration of his Friends' Housing for the Aged shows, can build in accordance with the other: the sad and mighty discordances of the apses, that music drear and grand of dying civilizations and the fate of mankind on a cooling star.

In that sense Venturi is, for all his own ironic disclaimers, one of the few American architects whose work seems to approach tragic stature in the tradition of Furness, Louis Sullivan, Wright, and Kahn. His being so suggests the power of successive generations, living in one place, to develop an intensity of meaning; so much of it is carried in Philadelphia: from Frank Furness to the young Sullivan, and on through Wilson Eyre and George Howe to Louis Kahn. Kahn is Venturi's closest mentor, as he has been for almost all the best young American architects and educators of the past decade, such as Giurgola, Moore, Vreeland, and Millard. The dialogue so developed, in which Aldo Van Eyck of Holland has also played an outstanding role, has surely contributed much to Venturi's development. Kahn's theory of "institutions" has been fundamental to all these architects, but Venturi himself avoids Kahn's structural preoccupations in favor of a more flexibly function-directed method which is closer to that of Alvar Aalto. Unlike his

writing, Venturi's design unfolds without strain. In it he is as facile as an architect of the Baroque and, in the same sense, as scenographic. (His project for the Roosevelt Memorial, probably the best, surely the most original of the entries, shows how serene and grand that scenographic talent can be.) There is none of Kahn's grim struggle in him, no profound agony of structural and functional opposites seeking expression. He is entirely at home with the particular and so offers the necessary opposition to the technological homogenizers who crowd our future. There is surely no quarrel here with Le Corbusier, or even with Mies, despite the universal regularity of the latter's forms. Many species of high quality can inhabit the same world. Such multiplicity is indeed the highest promise of the modern age to mankind, far more intrinsic to its nature than the superficial conformity or equally arbitrary packaging which its first stages suggest and which are so eagerly embraced by superficial designers.

The essential point is that Venturi's philosophy and design are humanistic, in which character his book resembles Geoffrey Scott's basic work, *The Architecture of Humanism,* of 1914. Therefore, it values before all else the actions of human beings and the effect of physical forms upon their spirit. In this, Venturi is an Italian architect of the great tradition—whose contact with that tradition came from art history at Princeton and a fellowship at the American Academy in Rome. But, as his Friends' Housing shows equally well, he is one of the very few architects whose thought parallels that of the Pop painters—and probably the first architect to perceive the usefulness and meaning of their forms. He has clearly learned a good deal from them during the past few years, though the major argument of this book was laid out in the late fifties and predates his knowledge of their work. Yet his "Main Street is almost all right," is just like their viewpoint, as is his instinct for changes of scale in small buildings and for the unsuspected life to be found in the common artifacts of mass culture when they are focused upon individually. The "Pop" in Le Corbusier's "Purism," as in that of the young Léger, should not be forgotten here, and it takes on renewed historical significance as its lesson of exploded scale and sharpened focus is learned once more. Again one has the feeling that Le Corbusier, painter and theorist that he was, would have best understood Venturi's alliance of visual method with intellectual intention.

It is significant in this regard that Venturi's ideas have so far stirred bitterest resentment among the more academic-minded of the Bauhaus generation—with its utter lack of irony, its spinsterish disdain for the popular culture but shaky grasp on any other, its incapacity to deal with monumental scale, its lip-service to technology, and its preoccupation with a rather prissily puristic aesthetic. Most of the Bauhaus design of the twenties, in buildings and furniture alike, can be distinguished by exactly those characteristics from Le Corbusier's more generous and varied forms of the period. Two strains in modern architecture seem to separate here, with Le Corbusier and Venturi now seen as working the same larger, more humane, architects' rather than "designers'" vein.

Venturi's projected City Hall for North Canton, Ohio, shows how his architecture also has a connection with the late work of Sullivan and so with the deepest untapped force of American vernacular experience as a whole. This is surely Venturi's largest achievement in American terms, that he opens our eyes again to the nature of things as they are in the United States—in the small town no less than in New York—and that out of our common, confused, mass-produced fabric he makes a solid architecture; he makes an art. In so doing he revives the popular traditions, and the particularized methodology, of the pre-Beaux Arts, pre-International Style, period. He thus completes that renewed connection with the whole of our past which Kahn's mature work had begun.

It is no wonder that few of the present crop of redevelopers can yet endure him. They, too, are much in the American grain, village boys with their noses pressed against the window of the candy store and with money to burn for the first time. So they are generally buying junk, fancy trash readymade by an army of architectural entrepreneurs, who portentously supply a spurious simplicity and the order of the tomb: the contemporary package, *par excellence*. Venturi looks both too complicated and too much like everyday for such people, who, in their architectural forms as in their social programs, would much prefer to gloss over a few of reality's more demanding faces. Hence, precisely because he recognizes and uses social phenomena as they exist, Venturi is the least "stylish" of architects, going always straight to the heart of the matter, working quickly without either fancy pretenses or vaporish asides. Although he has learned from Mannerist architec-

ture, his own buildings are in no sense "mannered," but surprisingly direct. After all, a television aerial at appropriate scale crowns his Friends' Housing, exactly as it fills—here neither good nor bad but a fact—our old people's lives. Whatever dignity may be in that, Venturi embodies, but he does not lie to us once concerning what the facts are. In the straightest sense, it is function that interests him, and the strong forms deriving from functional expression. Unlike too many architects of this generation, he is never genteel.

It is no wonder that Venturi's buildings have not found ready acceptance; they have been both too new and, for all their "accommodation" of complexity, too truly simple and unassuming for this affluent decade. They have refused to make much out of nothing, to indulge in flashy gestures, or to pander to fashion. They have been the product of a deeply systematic analysis in programmatic and visual terms and have therefore required a serious reorientation in all our thinking. Hence the symbolic image which prepares our eyes to see them has not yet been formed. This book may help in that regard. I believe that the future will value it among the few basic texts of our time—one which, despite its anti-heroic lack of pretension and its shift of perspective from the Champs-Elysées to Main Street, still picks up a fundamental dialogue begun in the twenties, and so connects us with the heroic generation of modern architecture once more.

Vincent Scully

Note to the Second Edition

There is no way to separate form from meaning; one cannot exist without the other. There can only be different critical assessments of the major ways through which form transmits meaning to the viewer: through empathy, said the nineteenth century, it embodies it; through the recognition of signs, say the linguists, it conveys it. Each side would agree that the relevant functioning agent in this process of the human brain is the memory: empathy and the identification of signs are both learned responses, the result of specific cultural experiences. The two modes of knowing and of deriving meaning from outside reality complement each other and are both at work in varying degrees in the shaping and the perception of all works of art.

In that sense, the making and the experience of architecture, as of every art, are always critical-historical acts, involving what the architect and the viewer have learned to distinguish and to image through their own relationship with life and things. It therefore follows that the strength and value of our contact with art will depend upon the quality of our historical knowledge. And it is obvious that knowledge instead of learning is the word which has to be employed here.

Venturi's two major books have been constructed along precisely these lines. They are both critical and historical. This one, the first, despite its significant introduction of several important modes of literary criticism into architectural writing, explores mainly the physical reaction to form and is thus basically empathetic in method. The second, *Learning from Las Vegas* (written with authors Denise Scott Brown and Steven Izenour), is primarily concerned with the function of sign in human art and is therefore fundamentally linguistic in its approach. Between them the two volumes, always impeccably visual in their argument, shape an impressive working aesthetic for contemporary architects.

At this distance, I feel doubly honored to have been invited to write the original introduction, which now seems to me not so well written as the book itself (edited by Marian Scully), but embarrassingly correct in its conclusions. I am especially pleased to have had the wit to assert in it that *Complexity and Contradiction* was "the most important writing on the making of architecture since Le Corbusier's *Vers une Architecture,* of 1923." Time has shown that this outrageous statement was nothing more than the unvarnished truth, and the critics who found it most amusing or infuriating at that moment now seem to spend a remarkable amount of energy quoting Venturi without acknowledgment, or chiding him for not going far enough, or showing that they themselves had really said it all long before. It doesn't matter much. What counts is that this brilliant, liberating book was published when it was. It provided architects and critics alike with more realistic and effective weapons, so that the breadth and relevance which the architectural dialogue has since achieved were largely initiated by it. Of primary interest are the newly eloquent buildings that have been inspired by its method, of which those by Venturi and Rauch have not surprisingly remained the most intellectually focused, archetypal, and distinguished. Once again, as when it sponsored the exhibition from which Hitchcock and Johnson's *The International Style* of 1932 derived, The Museum of Modern Art started something important when it backed this book.

V.S.
April, 1977

This book is both an attempt at architectural criticism and an apologia—an explanation, indirectly, of my work. Because I am a practicing architect, my ideas on architecture are inevitably a by-product of the criticism which accompanies working, and which is, as T. S. Eliot has said, of "capital importance . . . in the work of creation itself. Probably, indeed, the larger part of the labour of sifting, combining, constructing, expunging, correcting, testing: this frightful toil is as much critical as creative. I maintain even that the criticism employed by a trained and skilled writer on his own work is the most vital, the highest kind of criticism . . ."[1] I write, then, as an architect who employs criticism rather than a critic who chooses architecture and this book represents a particular set of emphases, a way of seeing architecture, which I find valid.

In the same essay Eliot discusses analysis and comparison as tools of literary criticism. These critical methods are valid for architecture too: architecture is open to analysis like any other aspect of experience, and is made more vivid by comparisons. Analysis includes the breaking up of architecture into elements, a technique I frequently use even though it is the opposite of the integration which is the final goal of art. However paradoxical it appears, and despite the suspicions of many Modern architects, such disintegration is a process present in all creation, and it is essential to understanding. Self-consciousness is necessarily a part of creation and criticism. Architects today are too educated to be either primitive or totally spontaneous, and architecture is too complex to be approached with carefully maintained ignorance.

As an architect I try to be guided not by habit but by a conscious sense of the past—by precedent, thoughtfully considered. The historical comparisons chosen are part of a continuous tradition relevant to my concerns. When Eliot writes about tradition, his comments are equally relevant to architecture, notwithstanding the more obvious changes in architectural methods due to technological innovations. "In English writing," Eliot says, "we seldom speak of tradition. . . . Seldom, perhaps, does the word appear except in a phrase of censure. If otherwise, it is vaguely approbative, with the implication, as to a work approved, of some pleasing archeological reconstruction. . . . Yet if the only form of tradition, of handing down, consisted in following the ways of the immediate generation before us in a blind or timid adherence to its successes, 'tradition' should be

positively discouraged. . . . Tradition is a matter of much wider significance. It cannot be inherited, and if you want it you must obtain it by great labour. It involves, in the first place, the historical sense, which we may call nearly indispensable to anyone who would continue to be a poet beyond his twenty-fifth year; and the historical sense involves perception, not only of the pastness of the past, but of its presence; the historical sense compels a man to write not merely with his own generation in his bones, but with a feeling that the whole of the literature of Europe . . . has a simultaneous existence and composes a simultaneous order. This historical sense, which is a sense of the timeless as well as of the temporal and of the timeless and temporal together, is what makes a writer traditional, and it is at the same time what makes a writer most acutely conscious of his place in time, of his own contemporaneity. . . . No poet, no artist of any kind, has his complete meaning alone."[2] I agree with Eliot and reject the obsession of Modern architects who, to quote Aldo van Eyck, "have been harping continually on what is different in our time to such an extent that they have lost touch with what is not different, with what is essentially the same."[3]

The examples chosen reflect my partiality for certain eras: Mannerist, Baroque, and Rococo especially. As Henry-Russell Hitchcock says, "there always exists a real need to re-examine the work of the past. There is, presumably, almost always a generic interest in architectural history among architects; but the aspects, or periods, of history that seem at any given time to merit the closest attention certainly vary with changing sensibilities."[4] As an artist I frankly write about what I like in architecture: complexity and contradiction. From what we find we like—what we are easily attracted to—we can learn much of what we really are. Louis Kahn has referred to "what a thing wants to be," but implicit in this statement is its opposite: what the architect wants the thing to be. In the tension and balance between these two lie many of the architect's decisions.

The comparisons include some buildings which are neither beautiful nor great, and they have been lifted abstractly from their historical context because I rely less on the idea of style than on the inherent characteristics of specific buildings. Writing as an architect rather than as a scholar, my historical view is that described by Hitchcock: "Once, of course, almost all investigation of the architecture of the past was in aid of its nominal reconstruction—an instrument of revivalism. That is no longer true, and there is little reason to fear that it will, in our time, become so again. Both the architects and the historian-critics of the early twentieth century, when they were not merely seeking in the past fresh ammunition for current polemical warfare, taught us to see all architecture, as it were, abstractly, false though such a limited vision probably is to the complex sensibilities that produced most of the great architecture of the past. When we re-examine—or discover—this or that aspect of earlier building production today, it is with no idea of repeating its forms, but rather in the expectation of feeding more amply new sensibilities that are wholly the product of the present. To the pure historian this may seem regrettable, as introducing highly subjective elements into what he believes ought to be objective studies. Yet the pure historian, more often than not, will eventually find himself moving in directions that have been already determined by more sensitive weathervanes." [5]

I make no special attempt to relate architecture to other things. I have not tried to "improve the connections between science and technology on the one hand, and the humanities and the social sciences on the other . . . and make of architecture a more human social art." [6] I try to talk about architecture rather than around it. Sir John Summerson has referred to the architects' obsession with "the importance, not of architecture, but of the *relation* of architecture to other things." [7] He has pointed out that in this century architects have substituted the "mischievous analogy" for the eclectic imitation of the nineteenth century, and have been staking a claim for architecture rather than producing architecture. [8] The result has been diagrammatic planning. The architect's ever diminishing power and his growing ineffectualness in shaping the whole environment can perhaps be reversed, ironically, by narrowing his concerns and concentrating on his own job. Perhaps then relationships and power will take care of themselves. I accept what seem to me architecture's inherent limitations, and attempt to concentrate on the difficult particulars within it rather than the easier abstractions about it ". . . because the arts belong (as the ancients said) to the practical and not the speculative intelligence, there is no surrogate for being on the job." [9]

This book deals with the present, and with the past in relation to the present. It does not attempt to be visionary except insofar as the future is inherent in the reality of the present. It is only indirectly polemical. Everything is said in the context of current architecture and consequently certain targets are attacked—in general, the limitations of orthodox Modern architecture and city planning, in particular, the platitudinous architects who invoke integrity, technology, or electronic programming as ends in architecture, the popularizers who paint "fairy stories over our chaotic reality" [10] and suppress those complexities and contradictions inherent in art and experience. Nevertheless, this book is an analysis of what seems to me true for architecture now, rather than a diatribe against what seems false.

Note to the Second Edition

I wrote this book in the early 1960's as a practicing architect responding to aspects of architectural theory and dogma of that time. The issues are different now, and I think the book might be read today for its general theories about architectural form but also as a particular document of its time, more historical than topical. For this reason the second part of the book, which covers the work of our firm up to 1966, is not expanded in this second edition.

I now wish the title had been *Complexity and Contradiction in Architectural Form,* as suggested by Donald Drew Egbert. In the early '60's, however, form was king in architectural thought, and most architectural theory focused without question on aspects of form. Architects seldom thought of symbolism in architecture then, and social issues came to dominate only in the second half of that decade. But in hindsight this book on form in architecture complements our focus on symbolism in architecture several years later in *Learning from Las Vegas*.

To rectify an omission in the acknowledgments of the first edition, I want to express my gratitude to Richard Krautheimer, who shared his insights on Roman Baroque architecture with us Fellows at the American Academy in Rome. I am grateful also to my friend Vincent Scully for his continued and very kind support of this book and of our work. I am happy that The Museum of Modern Art is enlarging the format of this edition so that the illustrations are now more readable.

Perhaps it is the fate of all theorists to view the ripples from their works with mixed feelings. I have sometimes felt more comfortable with my critics than with those who have agreed with me. The latter have often misapplied or exaggerated the ideas and methods of this book to the point of parody. Some have said the ideas are fine but don't go far enough. But most of the thought here was intended to be suggestive rather than dogmatic, and the method of historical analogy can be taken only so far in architectural criticism. Should an artist go all the way with his or her philosophies?

R.V.
April, 1977

1. Nonstraightforward Architecture: A Gentle Manifesto

I like complexity and contradiction in architecture. I do not like the incoherence or arbitrariness of incompetent architecture nor the precious intricacies of picturesqueness or expressionism. Instead, I speak of a complex and contradictory architecture based on the richness and ambiguity of modern experience, including that experience which is inherent in art. Everywhere, except in architecture, complexity and contradiction have been acknowledged, from Gödel's proof of ultimate inconsistency in mathematics to T. S. Eliot's analysis of "difficult" poetry and Joseph Albers' definition of the paradoxical quality of painting.

But architecture is necessarily complex and contradictory in its very inclusion of the traditional Vitruvian elements of commodity, firmness, and delight. And today the wants of program, structure, mechanical equipment, and expression, even in single buildings in simple contexts, are diverse and conflicting in ways previously unimaginable. The increasing dimension and scale of architecture in urban and regional planning add to the difficulties. I welcome the problems and exploit the uncertainties. By embracing contradiction as well as complexity, I aim for vitality as well as validity.

Architects can no longer afford to be intimidated by the puritanically moral language of orthodox Modern architecture. I like elements which are hybrid rather than "pure," compromising rather than "clean," distorted rather than "straightforward," ambiguous rather than "articulated," perverse as well as impersonal, boring as well as "interesting," conventional rather than "designed," accommodating rather than excluding, redundant rather than simple, vestigial as well as innovating, inconsistent and equivocal rather than direct and clear. I am for messy vitality over obvious unity. I include the non sequitur and proclaim the duality.

I am for richness of meaning rather than clarity of meaning; for the implicit function as well as the explicit function. I prefer "both-and" to "either-or," black and white, and sometimes gray, to black or white. A valid architecture evokes many levels of meaning and combinations of focus: its space and its elements become readable and workable in several ways at once.

But an architecture of complexity and contradiction has a special obligation toward the whole: its truth must be in its totality or its implications of totality. It must embody the difficult unity of inclusion rather than the easy unity of exclusion. More is not less.

2. Complexity and Contradiction vs. Simplification or Picturesqueness

Orthodox Modern architects have tended to recognize complexity insufficiently or inconsistently. In their attempt to break with tradition and start all over again, they idealized the primitive and elementary at the expense of the diverse and the sophisticated. As participants in a revolutionary movement, they acclaimed the newness of modern functions, ignoring their complications. In their role as reformers, they puritanically advocated the separation and exclusion of elements, rather than the inclusion of various requirements and their juxtapositions. As a forerunner of the Modern movement, Frank Lloyd Wright, who grew up with the motto "Truth against the World," wrote: "Visions of simplicity so broad and far-reaching would open to me and such building harmonies appear that . . . would change and deepen the thinking and culture of the modern world. So I believed." [11] And Le Corbusier, co-founder of Purism, spoke of the "great primary forms" which, he proclaimed, were "distinct . . . and without ambiguity." [12] Modern architects with few exceptions eschewed ambiguity.

But now our position is different: "At the same time that the problems increase in quantity, complexity, and difficulty they also change faster than before," [13] and require an attitude more like that described by August Heckscher: "The movement from a view of life as essentially simple and orderly to a view of life as complex and ironic is what every individual passes through in becoming mature. But certain epochs encourage this development; in them the paradoxical or dramatic outlook colors the whole intellectual scene. . . . Amid simplicity and order rationalism is born, but rationalism proves inadequate in any period of upheaval. Then equilibrium must be created out of opposites. Such inner peace as men gain must represent a tension among contradictions and uncertainties. . . . A feeling for paradox allows seemingly dissimilar things to exist side by side, their very incongruity suggesting a kind of truth." [14]

Rationalizations for simplification are still current, however, though subtler than the early arguments. They are expansions of Mies van der Rohe's magnificent paradox, "less is more." Paul Rudolph has clearly stated the implications of Mies' point of view: "All problems can never be solved. . . . Indeed it is a characteristic of the twentieth century that architects are highly selective in determining which problems they want to solve. Mies, for instance, makes wonderful buildings only because he ignores many aspects of a building. If he solved more problems, his buildings would be far less potent." [15]

The doctrine "less is more" bemoans complexity and justifies exclusion for expressive purposes. It does, indeed, permit the architect to be "highly selective in determining which problems [he wants] to solve." But if the architect must be "committed to his particular way of seeing the universe," [15] such a commitment surely means that the architect determines how problems should be solved, not that he can determine which of the problems he will solve. He can exclude important considerations only at the risk of separating architecture from the experience of life and the needs of society. If some problems prove insoluble, he can express this: in an inclusive rather than an exclusive kind of architecture there is room for the fragment, for contradiction, for improvisation, and for the tensions these produce. Mies' exquisite pavilions have had valuable implications for architecture, but their selectiveness of content and language is their limitation as well as their strength.

I question the relevance of analogies between pavilions and houses, especially analogies between Japanese pavilions and recent domestic architecture. They ignore the real complexity and contradiction inherent in the domestic program—the spatial and technological possibilities as well as the need for variety in visual experience. Forced simplicity results in oversimplification. In the Wiley House, for instance (1), in contrast to his glass house (2), Philip Johnson attempted to go beyond the simplicities of the elegant pavilion. He explicitly separated and articulated the enclosed "private functions" of living on a ground floor pedestal, thus separating them from the open social functions in the modular pavilion above. But even here the building becomes a diagram of an oversimplified program for living—an abstract theory of either-or. Where simplicity cannot work, simpleness results. Blatant simplification means bland architecture. Less is a bore.

The recognition of complexity in architecture does not negate what Louis Kahn has called "the desire for simplicity." But aesthetic simplicity which is a satisfaction to the mind derives, when valid and profound, from inner complexity. The Doric temple's simplicity to the eye is achieved through the famous subtleties and precision of its distorted geometry and the contradictions and tensions inherent in its order. The Doric temple could achieve apparent simplicity through real complexity. When complexity disappeared, as in the late temples, blandness replaced simplicity.

1. Johnson. Wiley House, New Canaan

2. Johnson. Glass House, New Canaan

Nor does complexity deny the valid simplification which is part of the process of analysis, and even a method of achieving complex architecture itself. "We oversimplify a given event when we characterize it from the standpoint of a given interest." [16] But this kind of simplification is a method in the analytical process of achieving a complex art. It should not be mistaken for a goal.

An architecture of complexity and contradiction, however, does not mean picturesqueness or subjective expressionism. A false complexity has recently countered the false simplicity of an earlier Modern architecture. It promotes an architecture of symmetrical picturesqueness—which Minoru Yamasaki calls "serene"—but it represents a new formalism as unconnected with experience as the former cult of simplicity. Its intricate forms do not reflect genuinely complex programs, and its intricate ornament, though dependent on industrial techniques for execution, is dryly reminiscent of forms originally created by handicraft techniques. Gothic tracery and Rococo rocaille were not only expressively valid in relation to the whole, but came from a valid showing-off of hand skills and expressed a vitality derived from the immediacy and individuality of the method. This kind of complexity through exuberance, perhaps impossible today, is the antithesis of "serene" architecture, despite the superficial resemblance between them. But if exuberance is not characteristic of our art, it is tension, rather than "serenity" that would appear to be so.

The best twentieth-century architects have usually rejected simplification—that is, simplicity through reduction—in order to promote complexity within the whole. The works of Alvar Aalto and Le Corbusier (who often disregards his polemical writings) are examples. But the characteristics of complexity and contradiction in their work are often ignored or misunderstood. Critics of Aalto, for instance, have liked him mostly for his sensitivity to natural materials and his fine detailing, and have considered his whole composition willful picturesqueness. I do not consider Aalto's Imatra church picturesque. By repeating in the massing the genuine complexity of the triple-divided plan and the acoustical ceiling pattern (3), this church represents a justifiable expressionism different from the willful picturesqueness of the haphazard structure and spaces of Giovanni Michelucci's recent church for the Autostrada (4).*Aalto's complexity is part of the program and structure of the whole rather than a device justified only by the

3. Aalto. Church, Vuoksenniska, near Imatra

desire for expression. Though we no longer argue over the primacy of form or function (which follows which?), we cannot ignore their interdependence.

The desire for a complex architecture, with its attendant contradictions, is not only a reaction to the banality or prettiness of current architecture. It is an attitude common in the Mannerist periods: the sixteenth century in Italy or the Hellenistic period in Classical art, and is also a continuous strain seen in such diverse architects as Michelangelo, Palladio, Borromini, Vanbrugh, Hawksmoor, Soane, Ledoux, Butterfield, some architects of the Shingle Style, Furness, Sullivan, Lutyens, and recently, Le Corbusier, Aalto, Kahn, and others.

Today this attitude is again relevant to both the medium of architecture and the program in architecture.

First, the medium of architecture must be re-examined if the increased scope of our architecture as well as the complexity of its goals is to be expressed. Simplified or superficially complex forms will not work. Instead, the variety inherent in the ambiguity of visual perception must once more be acknowledged and exploited.

Second, the growing complexities of our functional problems must be acknowledged. I refer, of course, to those programs, unique in our time, which are complex because of their scope, such as research laboratories, hospitals, and particularly the enormous projects at the scale of city and regional planning. But even the house, simple in scope, is complex in purpose if the ambiguities of contemporary experience are expressed. This contrast between the means and the goals of a program is significant. Although the means involved in the program of a rocket to get to the moon, for instance, are almost infinitely complex, the goal is simple and contains few contradictions; although the means involved in the program and structure of buildings are far simpler and less sophisticated technologically than almost any engineering project, the purpose is more complex and often inherently ambiguous.

*I have visited Giovanni Michelucci's Church of the Autostrada since writing these words, and I now realize it is an extremely beautiful and effective building. I am therefore sorry I made this unsympathetic comparison.

4. Michelucci. Church of the Autostrada, near Florence

While the second classification of complexity and contradiction in architecture relates to form and content as manifestations of program and structure, the first concerns the medium and refers to a paradox inherent in perception and the very process of meaning in art: the complexity and contradiction that results from the juxtaposition of what an image is and what it seems. Joseph Albers calls "the discrepancy between physical fact and psychic effect" a contradiction which is "the origin of art." And, indeed, complexity of meaning, with its resultant ambiguity and tension, has been characteristic of painting and amply recognized in art criticism. Abstract Expressionism acknowledges perceptual ambiguity, and the basis of Optical Art is shifting juxtapositions and ambiguous dualities relating to form and expression. Pop painters, too, have employed ambiguity to create paradoxical content as well as to exploit perceptual possibilities.

In literature, too, critics have been willing to accept complexity and contradiction in their medium. As in architectural criticism, they refer to a Mannerist era, but unlike most architectural critics, they also acknowledge a "mannerist" strain continuing through particular poets, and some, indeed, for a long time have emphasized the qualities of contradiction, paradox, and ambiguity as basic to the medium of poetry, just as Albers does with painting.

Eliot called the art of the Elizabethans "an impure art," [17] in which complexity and ambiguity are exploited: "in a play of Shakespeare," he said, "you get several levels of significance" [18] where, quoting Samuel Johnson, "the most heterogeneous ideas are yoked together by violence." [19] And elsewhere he wrote: "The case of John Webster . . . will provide an interesting example of a very great literary and dramatic genius directed towards chaos." [20] Other critics, for example, Kenneth Burke, who refers to "plural interpretation" and "planned incongruity," have analyzed elements of paradox and ambiguity in the structure and meaning of other poetry besides that of the seventeenth century metaphysical poets and those modern poets who have been influenced by them.

Cleanth Brooks justifies the expression of complexity and contradiction by their necessity as the very essence of art: "Yet there are better reasons than that of rhetorical vainglory that have induced poet after poet to choose ambiguity and paradox rather than plain discursive simplicity. It is not enough for the poet to analyze his experience as the scientist does, breaking it up into parts, distinguishing part from part, classifying the various parts. His task is finally to unify experience. He must return to us the unity of the experience itself as man knows it in his own experience. . . . If the poet . . . must perforce dramatize the oneness of the experience, even though paying tribute to its diversity, then his use of paradox and ambiguity is seen as necessary. He is not simply trying to spice up, with a superficially exciting or mystifying rhetoric the old stale stockpot. . . . He is rather giving us an insight which preserves the unity of experience and which, at its higher and more serious levels, triumphs over the apparently contradictory and conflicting elements of experience by unifying them into a new pattern." [21]

And in *Seven Types of Ambiguity* William Empson "dared to treat what [had] . . . been regarded as a deficiency in poetry, imprecision of meaning, as poetry's chief virtue . . ." [22] Empson documents his theory by readings from Shakespeare, "the supreme ambiguist, not so much from the confusion of his ideas and the muddle of his text, as some scholars believe, as simply from the power and complexity of his mind and art." [23]

Ambiguity and tension are everywhere in an architecture of complexity and contradiction. Architecture is form *and* substance—abstract *and* concrete—and its meaning derives from its interior characteristics and its particular context. An architectural element is perceived as form *and* structure, texture *and* material. These oscillating relationships, complex and contradictory, are the source of the ambiguity and tension characteristic to the medium of architecture. The conjunction "or" with a question mark can usually describe ambiguous relationships. The Villa Savoye (5): is it a square plan or not? The size of Vanbrugh's fore-pavilions at Grimsthorpe (6) in relation to the back pavilions is ambiguous from a distance: are they near or far, big or small? Bernini's pilasters on the Palazzo di Propaganda Fide (7): are they positive pilasters or negative panel divisions? The ornamental cove in the Casino di Pio IV in the Vatican (8) is perverse: is it more wall or more vault? The central dip in Lutyens' façade at Nashdom (9) facilitates skylighting: is the resultant duality resolved or not? Luigi Moretti's apartments on the Via Parioli in Rome (10): are they one building with a split or two buildings joined?

The calculated ambiguity of expression is based on the

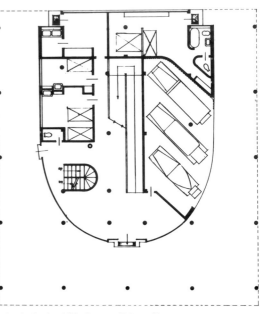

5. Le Corbusier. Villa Savoye, Poissy. Plan

6. Vanbrugh. Grimsthorpe, Lincolnshire

8. Ligorio. Casino di Pio IV, Vatican, Rome

7. Bernini. Façade, Palazzo di Propaganda Fide, Rome. Elevation

9. Lutyens. Nashdom, Taplow

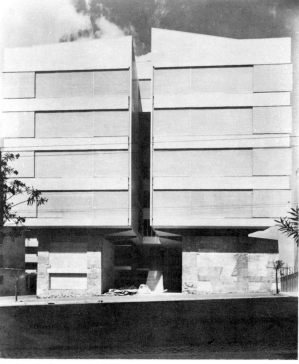

10. Moretti. Apartment Building, Via Parioli, Rome

confusion of experience as reflected in the architectural program. This promotes richness of meaning over clarity of meaning. As Empson admits, there is good and bad ambiguity: ". . . [ambiguity] may be used to convict a poet of holding muddled opinions rather than to praise the complexity of the order of his mind." [24] Nevertheless, according to Stanley Edgar Hyman, Empson sees ambiguity as "collecting precisely at the points of greatest poetic effectiveness, and finds it breeding a quality he calls 'tension' which we might phrase as the poetic impact itself." [25] These ideas apply equally well to architecture.

4. Contradictory Levels:
The Phenomenon of "Both-And" in Architecture

Contradictory levels of meaning and use in architecture involve the paradoxical contrast implied by the conjunctive "yet." They may be more or less ambiguous. Le Corbusier's Shodhan House (11) is closed yet open—a cube, precisely closed by its corners, yet randomly opened on its surfaces; his Villa Savoye (12) is simple outside yet complex inside. The Tudor plan of Barrington Court (13) is symmetrical yet asymmetrical; Guarini's Church of the Immaculate Conception in Turin (14) is a duality in plan and yet a unity; Sir Edwin Lutyens' entrance gallery at Middleton Park (15, 16) is directional space, yet it terminates at a blank wall; Vignola's façade for the pavilion at Bomarzo (17) contains a portal, yet it is a blank portico; Kahn's buildings contain crude concrete yet polished grantite; an urban street is directional as a route yet static as a place. This series of conjunctive "yets" describes an architecture of contradiction at varying levels of program and structure. None of these ordered contradictions represents a search for beauty, but neither as paradoxes, are they caprice.

Cleanth Brooks refers to Donne's art as "having it both ways" but, he says, "most of us in this latter day, cannot. We are disciplined in the tradition either-or, and lack the mental agility—to say nothing of the maturity of attitude—which would allow us to indulge in the finer distinctions and the more subtle reservations permitted by the tradition of both-and."[26] The tradition "either-or" has characterized orthodox modern architecture: a sun screen is probably nothing else; a support is seldom an enclosure; a wall is not violated by window penetrations but is totally interrupted by glass; program functions are exaggeratedly articulated into wings or segregated separate pavilions. Even "flowing space" has implied being outside when inside, and inside when outside, rather than both at the same time. Such manifestations of articulation and clarity are foreign to an architecture of complexity and contradiction, which tends to include "both-and" rather than exclude "either-or."

If the source of the both-and phenomenon is contradiction, its basis is hierarchy, which yields several levels of meanings among elements with varying values. It can include elements that are both good and awkward, big and little, closed and open, continuous and articulated, round and square, structural and spatial. An architecture which includes varying levels of meaning breeds ambiguity and tension.

11. Le Corbusier. Shodhan House, Ahmedabad

12. Le Corbusier. Villa Savoye, Poissy

23

13. Barrington Court, Somerset. Plan

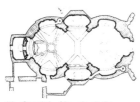

14. Guarini. Church of the Immaculate Conception, Turin. Plan

15. Lutyens. Middleton Park, Oxfordshire. Plan

16. Lutyens. Middleton Park, Oxfordshire

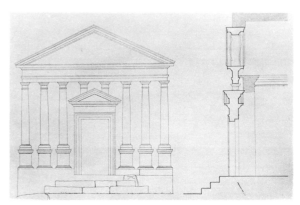

17. Vignola. Pavilion, Bomarzo. Elevation

Most of the examples will be difficult to "read," but abstruse architecture is valid when it reflects the complexities and contradictions of content and meaning. Simultaneous perception of a multiplicity of levels involves struggles and hesitations for the observer, and makes his perception more vivid.

Examples which are both good and bad at the same time will perhaps in one way explain Kahn's enigmatic remark: "architecture must have bad spaces as well as good spaces." Apparent irrationality of a part will be justified by the resultant rationality of the whole, or characteristics of a part will be compromised for the sake of the whole. The decisions for such valid compromises are one of the chief tasks of the architect.

In Hawksmoor's St. George-in-the-East (18) the exaggerated keystones over the aisle windows are wrong in relation to the part: when seen close-up they are too big in relation to the opening they span. When seen farther back, however, in the context of the whole composition, they are expressively right in size and scale. Michelangelo's enormous rectangular openings in the attic story of the rear façade of St. Peter's (19) are wider than they are high, so that they must be spanned the long way. This is perverse in relation to the spanning limitations of masonry, which dictate in Classical architecture that big openings, such as these, be vertically proportioned. But because one usually expects vertical proportions, the longitudinal spanning expresses validly and vividly their *relative* smallness.

The main stair in Frank Furness' Pennsylvania Academy of the Fine Arts in Philadelphia (20) is too big in relation to its immediate surroundings. It lands on a space narrower than its width, and faces an opening narrower than its width. Furthermore, the opening is bisected by a post. But this stair is ceremonial and symbolic as well as functional, and it relates to the hall immediately beyond the opening, to the whole building, and to the great scale of Broad Street outside. The outer thirds of Michelangelo's stair in the Laurentian Library vestibule (21) are abruptly chopped off and lead virtually nowhere: it is similarly wrong in the relation of its size to its space, and yet right in relation to the whole context of the spaces beyond.

Vanbrugh's end bays in the central pavilion of the entrance façade of Blenheim Palace (22) are incorrect because they are bisected by a pilaster: this fragmentation produces a duality which decreases their unity. Their very

20. Furness. Pennsylvania Academy of the Fine Arts, Philadelphia

18. Hawksmoor. St. George-in-the-East, London

19. Michelangelo. Rear Façade, St. Peter's, Rome

21. Michelangelo. Laurentian Library, Florence. Plan

25

incompleteness, however, reinforces by contrast the center bay and increases the overall unity of this complex composition. The pavilions which flanked the château at Marly (23) contained a similar paradox. The compositional duality of their two-bay façades lacks unity, but reinforces the unity of the whole complex. Their own incompleteness implied the dominance of the château itself and the completeness of the whole.

The basilica, which has mono-directional space, and the central-type church, which has omnidirectional space, represent alternating traditions in Western church plans. But another tradition has accommodated churches which are both-and, in answer to spatial, structural, programmatic, and symbolic needs. The Mannerist elliptical plan of the sixteenth century is both central and directional. Its culmination is Bernini's Sant' Andrea al Quirinale (24), whose main directional axis contradictorily spans the short axis. Nikolaus Pevsner has shown how pilasters rather than open chapels bisect both ends of the transverse axis of the side walls, thereby reinforcing the short axis toward the altar. Borromini's chapel in the Propaganda Fide (25) is a directional hall in plan, but its alternating bays counteract this effect: a large bay dominates the small end; a small bay bisects the center of the long wall. The rounded corners, as well, begin to imply a continuity of enclosure and a central-type plan. (These characteristics occur in the courtyard of San Carlo alle Quattro Fontane too.) And the diagonal gridlike ribs in the ceiling indicate a multidirectional structure as much like a dome as a vault. Hagia Sophia in Istanbul is equivocal in a similar way. Its central dome on the square bay with pendentives implies a central type church, but its two apses with half-domes begin to set up a longitudinal axis in the tradition of the directional basilica. The horseshoe plan of the Baroque and neo-Baroque opera house focuses on the stage and the center of the auditorium. The central focus of the elliptical plan is usually reflected in the ornamental ceiling pattern and the enormous central chandelier; the focus toward the stage in the directional distortion of the ellipse and partitions between the surrounding boxes as well as in the interruption of the stage itself, of course, and the seating in the pit. This reflects the dual focus in the program of the gala theatre: the performance and the audience.

Borromini's San Carlo alle Quattro Fontane (26) abounds in ambiguous manifestations of both-and. The

22. Vanbrugh. Blenheim Palace, Oxfordshire

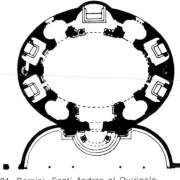

23. Hardouin-Mansart. Pavilion, Marly. Elevation

24. Bernini. Sant' Andrea al Quirinale, Rome. Plan

25. Borromini. Church of the Re Magi, Palazzo di Propaganda Fide, Rome

27. Borromini. San Carlo alle Quattro Fontane, Rome

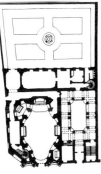

26. Borromini. San Carlo alle Quattro Fontane,
    Rome. Plan

almost equal treatment of the four wings implied in the plan suggests a Greek cross, but the wings are distorted toward a dominant east-west axis, thus suggesting a Latin cross, while the fluid continuity of the walls indicates a distorted circular plan. Rudolf Wittkower has analyzed similar contradictions in section. The pattern of the ceiling in the articulations of its complex mouldings suggests a dome on pendentives over the crossing of a Greek cross (27). The shape of the ceiling in its overall continuity distorts these elements into parodies of themselves, and suggests rather a dome generated from an undulating wall. These distorted elements are both continuous and articulated. At another scale, shape and pattern play similarly contradictory roles. For example, the profile of the Byzantine capital (28) makes it seem continuous, but the texture and vestigial patterns of volutes and acanthus leaves articulate the parts.

The pedimented porch of Nicholas Hawksmoor's St. George, Bloomsbury (29), and the overall shape of its plan (30) imply a dominant axis north and south. The west entrance and tower, the interior configuration of balconies, and the east apse (which contained the altar) all suggest an equally dominant counter axis. By means of contrary elements and distorted positions this church expresses both the contrasts between the back, front, and sides of the Latin cross plan and the duo-directional axes of a Greek cross plan. These contradictions, which resulted from particular site and orientation conditions, support a richness and tension lacking in many purer compositions.

The domed basilica of Vierzehnheiligen (31) has a central altar under a major dome in the nave. Nikolaus Pevsner has vividly contrasted its series of domes, which are distorted and superimposed on the Latin cross plan, with the conventional placing of a single dome at the crossing. This is a Latin cross church, which is also a central-type church because of the unusual position of the altar and the central dome. Other late Baroque churches juxtapose the square and the circle. Bernardo Vittone's elements—ambiguously pendentives or squinches—in the nave of S. Maria di Piazza in Turin (32) support what is both a dome and a square lantern. Hawksmoor juxtaposes mouldings in rectangular and elliptical patterns on the ceilings of some of his churches. They create contradictory expressions of both central and directional-type churches. In some rooms of the Palazzo di Propaganda Fide (33) a straddling

28. Capital, Hagia Sophia, Istanbul

29. Hawksmoor. St. George, Bloomsbury

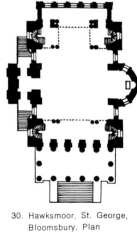

30. Hawksmoor. St. George, Bloomsbury. Plan

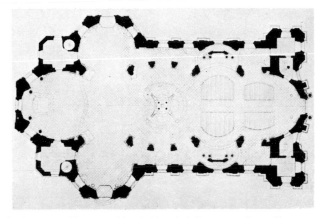

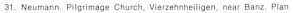
31. Neumann. Pilgrimage Church, Vierzehnheiligen, near Banz. Plan

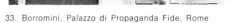
33. Borromini. Palazzo di Propaganda Fide, Rome

32. Vittone. S. Maria di Piazza, Turin

34. Wren. St. Stephen Walbrook, London. Interior perspective

arch in the corners allows the space to be rectangular below and continuous above. This is similar to Wren's ceiling configuration in St. Stephen Walbrook (34).

In the ceilings of his secular chambers (35) Sir John Soane glories in spaces and structures both rectangular and curvilinear, and domed and vaulted. His methods include complex combinations of vestigial structural shapes resembling squinches and pendentives, oculi, and groins. Soane's Museum (36) employs a vestigial element in another dimension: the partition in the form of suspended arches, meaningless structurally yet meaningful spatially, defines rooms at once open and closed.

The façade of the cathedral at Murcia (37) employs what has been called inflection to promote largeness yet smallness. The broken pediments above the shafts are inflected toward each other to help suggest an enormous portal, appropriate spatially to the plaza below and symbolically to the region beyond. Storied orders within the shafts, however, accommodate the scale of the immediate conditions of the building itself and its setting. Bigness and smallness are expressed at once in a characteristic Shingle Style stair through distortion in width and direction. The risers and treads remain constant, of course, but the widening of the run at the bottom accommodates the spacious living-room hall below, while the narrower run at the top relates to the narrower hall above.

Precast concrete construction can be continuous yet fragmentary, flowing in profile yet surfaced with joints. The contours of its profiles between columns and beams can designate the continuity of the structural system, but the pattern of its grouted joints can designate the fragmented method of its erection.

The tower of Christ Church, Spitalfields (38), is a manifestation of both-and at the scale of the city. Hawksmoor's tower is both a wall and a tower. Toward the bottom the vista is terminated by the extension of its walls into kinds of buttresses (39) perpendicular to the approaching street. They are seen from only one direction. The top evolves into a spire, which is seen from all sides, spatially and symbolically dominating the skyline of the parish. In the Bruges Cloth Hall (40) the scale of the building relates to the immediate square, while the violently disproportionate scale of the tower above relates to the whole town. For similar reasons the big sign sits on top of the Philadelphia Savings Fund Society Building, and yet

35. Soane. Court of Exchequer, Palace of Westminster, London. Interior perspective

36. Soane. Soane House and Museum, Lincoln's Inn Fields, London. Interior perspective

37. Murcia Cathedral

it is invisible from below (41). The Arc de Triomphe also has contrasting functions. Seen diagonally from the radial approaches other than the Champs Elysées, it is a sculptural termination. Seen perpendicularly from the axis of the Champs Elysées, it is spatially and symbolically both a termination and a portal. Later I shall analyze some organized contradictions between front and back. But here I shall mention the Karlskirche in Vienna (42), whose exterior contains elements both of the basilica in its façade and of the central-type church in its body. A convex form in the back was required by the interior program; the urban space required a larger scale and a straight façade in front. The disunity that exists from the point of view of the building itself is contradicted when the building is seen in relation to the scale and the space of the neighborhood.

The double meanings inherent in the phenomenon both-and can involve metamorphosis as well as contradiction. I have described how the omni-directional spire of the tower of Christ Church, Spitalfields, evolves into a directional pavilion at its base, but a perceptual rather than a formal kind of change in meaning is possible. In equivocal relationships one contradictory meaning usually dominates another, but in complex compositions the relationship is not always constant. This is especially true as the observer moves through or around a building, and by extension through a city: at one moment one meaning can be perceived as dominant; at another moment a different meaning seems paramount. In St. George, Bloomsbury (30), for instance, the contradictory axes inside become alternatingly dominant or recessive as the observer moves within them, so that the same space changes meaning. Here is another dimension of "space, time and architecture" which involves the multiple focus.

38. Hawksmoor. Christ Church, Spitalfields

39. Hawksmoor. Christ Church, Spitalfields

41. Howe and Lescaze. Philadelphia Savings Fund Society Building

40. Cloth Hall and Belfry, Bruges

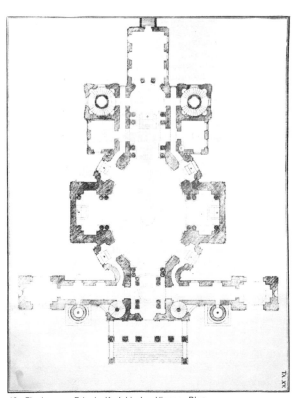

42. Fischer von Erlach. Karlskirche, Vienna. Plan

5. Contradictory Levels Continued: The Double-Functioning Element

The "double-functioning" [27] element and "both-and" are related, but there is a distinction: the double-functioning element pertains more to the particulars of use and structure, while both-and refers more to the relation of the part to the whole. Both-and emphasizes double meanings over double-functions. But before I talk about the double-functioning element, I want to mention the multifunctioning building. By this term I mean the building which is complex in program and form, yet strong as a whole—the complex unity of Le Corbusier's La Tourette or the Palace of Justice at Chandigarh in contrast to the multiplicities and articulations of his Palace of the Soviets project or the Armée du Salut in Paris. The latter approach separates functions into interlocking wings or connected pavilions. It has been typical of orthodox Modern architecture. The incisive separations of the pavilions in Mies' design for the urban Illinois Institute of Technology can be understood as an extreme development of it.

Mies' and Johnson's Seagram Building excludes functions other than offices (except on the ground floor in back), and by using a similar wall pattern camouflages the fact that at the top there is a different kind of space for mechanical equipment. Yamasaki's project for The World Trade Center in New York even more exaggeratedly simplifies the form of an enormous complex. The typical office skyscrapers of the '20's differentiate, rather than camouflage, their mechanical equipment space at the top through architecturally ornamental forms. While Lever House includes differently-functioning spaces at the bottom, it exaggeratedly separates them by a spatial shadow joint. In contrast, one exceptional Modern building, the P.S.F.S. (41), gives positive expression to the variety and complexity of its program. It integrates a shop on the first floor and a big bank on the second with offices above and special rooms at the top. These varieties of functions and scales (including the enormous advertising sign at the top) work within a compact whole. Its curving façade, which contrasts with the rectangularity of the rest of the building, is not just a cliché of the '30's, because it has an urban function. At the lower pedestrian level it directs space around the corner.

The multifunctioning building in its extreme form becomes the Ponte Vecchio or Chenonceaux or the Futurist projects of Sant' Elia. Each contains within the whole contrasting scales of movement besides complex functions.

Le Corbusier's Algerian project, which is an apartment house and a highway, and Wright's late projects for Pittsburgh Point and Baghdad, correspond to Kahn's viaduct architecture and Fumihiko Maki's "collective form." All of these have complex and contradictory hierarchies of scale and movement, structure, and space within a whole. These buildings are buildings and bridges at once. At a larger scale: a dam is also a bridge, the loop in Chicago is a boundary as well as a circulation system, and Kahn's street "wants to be a building."

There are justifications for the multifunctioning room as well as the multifunctioning building. A room can have many functions at the same time or at different times. Kahn prefers the gallery because it is directional and nondirectional, a corridor and room at once. And he recognizes the changing complexities of specific functions by differentiating rooms in a general way through a hierarchy of size and quality, calling them servant and major spaces, directional and nondirectional spaces, and other designations more generic than specific. As in his project for the Trenton Community Center, these spaces end by paralleling in a more complex way the pre-eighteenth century configurations of rooms en suite. The idea of corridors and rooms each with a single function for convenience originated in the eighteenth century. Is not Modern architecture's characteristic separation and specialization of program functions within the building through built-in furniture an extreme manifestation of this idea? Kahn by implication questions such rigid specialization and limited functionalism. In this context, "form evokes function."

The multifunctioning room is a possibly truer answer to the Modern architect's concern with flexibility. The room with a generic rather than a specific purpose, and with movable furniture rather than movable partitions, promotes a perceptual flexibility rather than a physical flexibility, and permits the toughness and permanence still necessary in our building. Valid ambiguity promotes useful flexibility.

The double-functioning element has been used infrequently in Modern architecture. Instead, Modern architecture has encouraged separation and specialization at all scales—in materials and structure as well as program and space. "The nature of materials" has precluded the multifunctioning material, or, inversely, the same form or surface for different materials. Wright's divergence from his master began, according to his autobiography, with Louis Sulli-

43. Rauschenberg. *Pilgrim*, 1960

44. Katsura Villa, Kyoto

van's indiscriminate application of his characteristic ornament to terra cotta, iron, wood, or brick. To Wright,
"appropriate designs for one material would not be appropriate for another material." [28] But the façade of Eero
Saarinen's dormitory at the University of Pennsylvania includes among its materials and structure vine-covered
grade, brick wall, and steel grille—yet the curving profile of
its form is continuous. Saarinen overcame the current obsession against using different materials in the same plane
or the same material for two different things. In Robert
Rauschenberg's painting, *Pilgrim* (43), the surface pattern
continues from the stretcher canvas to the actual chair in
front of it, making ambiguous the distinction between the
painting and the furniture, and on another level, the work
of art in a room. A contradiction between levels of function and meaning is recognized in these works, and the
medium is strained.

But to the structural purist, as well as the organicist,
the double-functioning structural form would be abhor-
rent because of the nonexact, ambiguous correspondence
between form and function, and form and structure. In
contrast, in the Katsura Villa (44) the bamboo rod in
tension and the wood post in compression are similar in
form. To the Modern architect, I think, the two would seem
sinisterly similar in section and size despite the current
inclination toward traditional Japanese design. The Renaissance pilaster (as well as other structural elements used in a
nonstructural way) can involve the phenomenon both-
and at several levels. It can be at the same time physically
structural or not, symbolically structural through association, and compositionally ornamental by promoting rhythm
and also complexity of scale in the giant order.

Besides specializing forms in relation to materials and
structure, Modern architecture separates and articulates elements. Modern architecture is never implicit. In promoting
the frame and the curtain wall, it has separated structure
from shelter. Even the walls of the Johnson Wax Building
are enclosing but not supporting. And in detailing, Modern
architecture has tended to glory in separation. Even the
flush joint is articulated, and the shadow joint predominates. The versatile element which does several things at
once is equally rare in Modern architecture. Significantly
the column is favored over the pier. In S. Maria in Cosmedin's nave (45) the column form results from its dominant, precise function as a point support. It can direct space

45. S. Maria in Cosmedin, Rome

only incidentally in relation to other columns or elements. But the alternating piers in the same nave are intrinsically double-functioning. They enclose and direct space as much as they support structure. The Baroque piers in the chapel at Frèsnes (46), residual as form and redundant as structure, are extreme examples of double-functioning elements which are structural and spatial at once.

Le Corbusier's and Kahn's double-functioning elements may be rare in our architecture. The brise-soleils in the Unité d'Habitation in Marseilles are structure and porches as well as sunscreens. (Are they wall segments, piers, or columns?) Kahn's clusters of columns and his open piers "harbor" space for equipment, and can manipulate natural light as well, like the rhythmically complex columns and pilasters of Baroque architecture. Like the open beams in the Richards Medical Center (47), these elements are neither structurally pure nor elegantly minimum in section. Instead, they are structural fragments inseparable from a greater spatial whole. It is valid to sense stresses in forms which are not purely structural, and a structural member can be more than incidentally spatial. (However, the columns and the stair towers in this building are separated and articulated in an orthodox manner.)

Flat plate construction consists of concrete slabs of constant depth and varied reinforcement, with irregularly placed columns without beams or caps. To maintain a constant depth, the number of reinforcing bars changes to accommodate the more concentrated structural loads in the constant, beamless section. This permits, in apartment houses especially, a constant ceiling profile for the spaces below in order to accommodate partitions. Flat plates are structurally impure: their section is not minimum. The demands of structural forces are compromised because of the demands of architectural space. Form follows function here in a contradictory way; substance follows structural function; profile follows spatial function.

In some Mannerist and Baroque masonry construction the pier, pilaster, and relieving arch about evenly make up a façade, and the resultant structure, like that of the Palazzo Valmarana (48), is bearing wall and frame at once. The relieving arches in the Pantheon (49), in this case not originally part of the visual expression, similarly generate a wall structurally double-functioning. In this context the Roman basilica, Gaudí's Sagrada Familia (50), and Palladio's Il Redentore (51) are totally different from the

46. Mansart. Chapel, Frèsnes. Plan

47. Kahn. Richards Medical Research Building, University of Pennsylvania, Philadelphia

48 Palladio. Palazzo Valmarana. Vicenza. Elevation

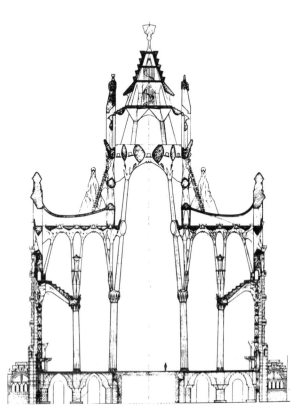

50. Gaudi. Church of the Sagrada Familia, Barcelona. Section

51. Palladio. Il Redentore, Venice

49. Pantheon, Rome. Perspective

52. St. Urban, Troyes

Gothic basilica (52). In contrast to the segregated flying buttress, the Roman countervault spans as well as buttresses, and Gaudí's subtle invention of the tilted pier-buttress supports the weight of the vault as well as buttresses the thrust in one continuous form. Palladio's buttresses are also broken pediments on the façade. A flying buttress at S. Chiara in Assisi forms a portal for the piazza as well as a support for the building.

The double-functioning element can be a detail. Mannerist and Baroque buildings abound in drip mouldings which become sills, windows which become niches, cornice ornaments which accommodate windows, quoin strips which are also pilasters, and architraves which make arches (53). The pilasters of Michelangelo's niches in the entrance of the Laurentian Library (54) also look like brackets. Borromini's mouldings in the rear façades of the Propaganda Fide (55) are both window frames and pediments. Lutyens' chimneys at Grey Walls (56) are literally sculptural entrance markers as well, a dado at Gledstone Hall (57) is an extension of a stair riser in the same room, and the stair landing at Nashdom is also a room.

The balloon frame, which has been traced by Siegfried Giedion, *becomes* on all levels. Structurally and visually it evolves from a separate frame to a skin which is both structural and sheltering: to the extent that it is made up of 2 x 4's, it is frame; to the extent that the 2 x 4's are small, close together, and braced and meshed by diagonal siding, it becomes skin. These intricate characteristics are evident in the way penetrations are made in it and in the way it is terminated. The balloon frame is another element in architecture which is several things at once. It represents a method between two pure extremes, which has evolved from each of them until it has characteristics of both.

Conventional elements in architecture represent one stage in an evolutionary development, and they contain in their changed use and expression some of their past meaning as well as their new meaning. What can be called the vestigial element parallels the double-functioning element. It is distinct from a superfluous element because it contains a double meaning. This is the result of a more or less ambiguous combination of the old meaning, called up by associations, with a new meaning created by the modified or new function, structural or programmatic, and the new context. The vestigial element discourages clarity of meaning; it promotes richness of meaning instead. It is a

53. Borromini. S. Maria dei Sette Dolori, Rome

54. Michelangelo, Laurentian Library, Florence

55. Borromini. Palazzo di Propaganda Fide, Rome

56. Lutyens. Grey Walls, Scotland

57. Lutyens. Gledstone Hall, Yorkshire

58. Ledoux. Project for a Gateway, Bourneville

59. Vanbrugh. Blenheim Palace, Oxfordshire

basis for change and growth in the city as manifest in remodeling which involves old buildings with new uses both programmatic and symbolic (like palazzi which become museums or embassies), and old street patterns with new uses and scales of movement. The paths of medieval fortification walls in European cities became boulevards in the nineteenth century; a section of Broadway is a piazza and a symbol rather than an artery to upper New York state. The ghost of Dock Street in Philadelphia's Society Hill, however, is a meaningless vestige rather than a working element resulting from a valid transition between the old and the new. I shall later refer to the vestigial element as it appears in Michelangelo's architecture and in what might be called Pop architecture.

The rhetorical element, like the double-functioning element, is infrequent in recent architecture. If the latter offends through its inherent ambiguity, rhetoric offends orthodox Modern architecture's cult of the minimum. But the rhetorical element is justified as a valid if outmoded means of expression. An element can seem rhetorical from one point of view, but if it is valid, at another level it enriches meaning by underscoring. In the project for a gateway at Bourneville by Ledoux (58), the columns in the arch are structurally rhetorical if not redundant. Expressively, however, they underscore the abstractness of the opening as a semicircle more than an arch, and they further define the opening as a gateway. As I have said, the stairway at the Pennsylvania Academy of the Fine Arts by Furness is too big in its immediate context, but appropriate as a gesture towards the outside scale and a sense of entry. The Classical portico is a rhetorical entrance. The stairs, columns, and pediment are juxtaposed upon the other-scale, real entrance behind. Paul Rudolph's entrance in the Art and Architecture Building at Yale is at the scale of the city; most people use the little door at the side in the stair tower.

Much of the function of ornament is rhetorical—like the use of Baroque pilasters for rhythm, and Vanbrugh's disengaged pilasters at the entrance to the kitchen court at Blenheim (59) which are an architectural fanfare. The rhetorical element which is also structural is rare in Modern architecture, although Mies has used the rhetorical I-beam with an assurance that would make Bernini envious.

6. Accommodation and the Limitations of Order: The Conventional Element

In short, that contradictions must be accepted.*

A valid order accommodates the circumstantial contradictions of a complex reality. It accommodates as well as imposes. It thereby admits "control *and* spontaneity," "correctness *and* ease"—improvisation within the whole. It tolerates qualifications and compromise. There are no fixed laws in architecture, but not everything will work in a building or a city. The architect must decide, and these subtle evaluations are among his principal functions. He must determine what must be made to work and what it is possible to compromise with, what will give in, and where and how. He does not ignore or exclude inconsistencies of program and structure within the order.

I have emphasized that aspect of complexity and contradiction which grows out of the medium more than the program of the building Now I shall emphasize the complexity and contradiction that develops from the program and reflects the inherent complexities and contradictions of living. It is obvious that in actual practice the two must be interrelated. Contradictions can represent the exceptional inconsistency that modifies the otherwise consistent order, or they can represent inconsistencies throughout the order as a whole. In the first case, the relationship between inconsistency and order accommodates circumstantial exceptions to the order, or it juxtaposes particular with general elements of order. Here you build an order up and then break it down, but break it from strength rather than from weakness. I have described this relationship as "contradiction accommodated." The relationship of inconsistency within the whole I consider a manifestation of "the difficult whole," which is discussed in the last chapter.

Mies refers to a need to "create order out of the desperate confusion of our time." But Kahn has said "by order I do not mean orderliness." Should we not resist bemoaning confusion? Should we not look for meaning in the complexities and contradictions of our times and acknowledge the limitations of systems? These, I think, are the two justifications for breaking order: the recognition of variety and confusion inside and outside, in program and environment, indeed, at all levels of experience; and the

* David Jones, *Epoch and Artist,* Chilmark Press, New York, 1959.

ultimate limitation of all orders composed by man. When circumstances defy order, order should bend or break: anomalies and uncertainties give validity to architecture.

Meaning can be enhanced by breaking the order; the exception points up the rule. A building with no "imperfect" part can have no perfect part, because contrast supports meaning. An artful discord gives vitality to architecture. You can allow for contingencies all over, but they cannot prevail all over. If order without expediency breeds formalism, expediency without order, of course, means chaos. Order must exist before it can be broken. No artist can belittle the role of order as a way of seeing a whole relevant to its own characteristics and context. "There is no work of art without a system" is Le Corbusier's dictum.

Indeed a propensity to break the order can justify exaggerating it. A valid formalism, or a kind of paper architecture in this context, compensates for distortions, expediencies, and exceptions in the circumstantial parts of the composition, or for violent superimpositions in juxtaposed contradictions. In recent architecture Le Corbusier in the Villa Savoye, for example, accommodates the exceptional circumstantial inconsistencies in an otherwise rigid, dominant order. But Aalto, in contrast to Le Corbusier, seems almost to create the order out of the inconsistencies, as can be seen in the Cultural Center at Wolfsburg. An historical example will perhaps help to illustrate this relation of order and exception. The appliqué of arches and pilasters on the Palazzo Tarugi (60) maintains itself against the sudden impositions of "whimsical" windows and asymmetrical voids. The exaggerated order, and therefore exaggerated unity, along with certain characteristics of scale, are what make the monumentality in the Italian palazzo and some of the work of Le Corbusier. The circumstantial oppositions in their compositions, however, are the secret of their kind of monumentality—that which is neither dry nor pompous. Although Aalto's order is not quite so easily grasped at first glance, it involves similar relationships of order and the circumstantial.

In engineering it is the bridge (61) that vividly expresses the play of exaggeratedly pure order against circumstantial inconsistencies. The direct, geometric order of the upper structure, derived from the sole, simple function of conveying vehicles on an even span, strongly contrasts with the exceptional accommodation of the structural order below, which through distortion—the expedient device of

60. Cangallo. Palazzo Tarugi, Montepulciano

61. Carè and Giannelli. Poggettone and Pecora Vecchia Viaducts, Autostrada del Sole, Bologna-Florence Section

elongated or shortened piers—accommodates the bridge to the uneven terrain of the ravine.

A play of order and compromise also supports the idea of renovation in building, and of evolution in city planning. Indeed, change in the program of existing buildings is a valid phenomenon and a major source of the contradiction I am endorsing. Many compositions that acknowledge circumstantial exceptions, like the Palazzo Tarugi, result from renovations that maintain an expresssion of the whole. Much of the richness of the Italian urban scene at eye level results from the tradition of modifying or modernizing every several generations the commercial ground floor interiors, for example, the frankly stylish contemporary bars, located in the frames of old palazzi. But the building's original order must be strong. A good deal of clutter has not managed to destroy the space of Grand Central Station but the introduction of one foreign element casts into doubt the entire effect of some modern buildings. Our buildings must survive the cigarette machine.

I have been referring to one level of order in architecture—that individual order that is related to the specific building it is part of. But there is convention in architecture, and convention can be another manifestation of an exaggeratedly strong order more general in scope. An architect should use convention and make it vivid. I mean he should use convention unconventionally. By convention I mean both the elements and methods of building. Conventional elements are those which are common in their manufacture, form, and use. I do not refer to the sophisticated

products of industrial design, which are usually beautiful, but to the vast accumulation of standard, anonymously designed products connected with architecture and construction, and also to commercial display elements which are positively banal or vulgar in themselves and are seldom associated with architecture.

The main justification for honky-tonk elements in architectural order is their very existence. They are what we have. Architects can bemoan or try to ignore them or even try to abolish them, but they will not go away. Or they will not go away for a long time, because architects do not have the power to replace them (nor do they know what to replace them with), and because these commonplace elements accommodate existing needs for variety and communication. The old clichés involving both banality and mess will still be the context of our new architecture, and our new architecture significantly will be the context for them. I am taking the limited view, I admit, but the limited view, which architects have tended to belittle, is as important as the visionary view, which they have tended to glorify but have not brought about. The short-term plan, which expediently combines the old and the new, must accompany the long-term plan. Architecture is evolutionary as well as revolutionary. As an art it will acknowledge what is and what ought to be, the immediate and the speculative.

Historians have shown how architects in the mid-nineteenth century tended to ignore or reject developments in technology when related to structure and methods as unconnected with architecture and unworthy of it; they substituted in turn Gothic Revivalism, Academic revivalism or the Handicraft Movement. Are we today proclaiming advanced technology, while excluding the immediate, vital if vulgar elements which are common to our architecture and landscape? The architect should accept the methods and the elements he already has. He often fails when he attempts per se the search for form hopefully new, and the research for techniques hopefully advanced. Technical innovations require investments in time and skills and money beyond the architect's reach, at least in our kind of society. The trouble with nineteenth century architects was not so much that they left innovation to the engineers as that they ignored the technical revolution developed by others. Present-day architects, in their visionary compulsion to invent new techniques, have neglected their obligation to be experts in existing conventions. The architect, of course, is responsible for the how as well as the what in his building, but his innovating role is primarily in the what; his experimentation is limited more to his organization of the whole than to technique in the parts. The architect selects as much as creates.

These are pragmatic reasons for using convention in architecture, but there are expressive justifications as well. The architect's main work is the organization of a unique whole through conventional parts and the judicious introduction of new parts when the old won't do. Gestalt psychology maintains that context contributes meaning to a part and change in context causes change in meaning. The architect thereby, through the organization of parts, creates meaningful contexts for them within the whole. Through unconventional organization of conventional parts he is able to create new meanings within the whole. If he uses convention unconventionally, if he organizes familiar things in an unfamiliar way, he is changing their contexts, and he can use even the cliché to gain a fresh effect. Familiar things seen in an unfamiliar context become perceptually new as well as old.

Modern architects have exploited the conventional element only in limited ways. If they have not totally rejected it as obsolete or banal, they have embraced it as symbolic of progressive industrial order. But they have seldom used the common element with a unique context in an uncommon way. Wright, for instance, almost always employed unique elements and unique forms, which represented his personal and innovating approach to architecture. Minor elements,

like hardware by Schlage or plumbing fixtures by Kohler of Kohler, which even Wright was unable to avoid using, read as unfortunate compromises within the particular order of his buildings, which is otherwise consistent.

Gropius in his early work, however, employed forms and elements based on a consistent industrial vocabulary. He thus recognized standardization and promoted his machine aesthetic. The inspiration for windows and stairways, for instance, came from current factory architecture, and these buildings look like factories. Latter-day Mies employs the structural elements of vernacular American industrial architecture and also those of Albert Kahn with unconscious irony: the elegant frame members are derived from standard steel manufacturers' catalogues; they are expressed as exposed structure but they are ornament on a fire-resistant frame; and they make up complex, closed spaces rather than the simple industrial spaces they were originally designed for.

It was Le Corbusier who juxtaposed objets trouvés and commonplace elements, such as the Thonet chair, the officer's chair, cast iron radiators, and other industrial objects, and the sophisticated forms of his architecture with any sense of irony. The nineteenth century statue of the Virgin within the window of the east wall of the Chapel at Ronchamp is a vestige from the former church which stood on the spot. Besides its symbolic value, it represents a banal object of sculpture vividly enhanced by its new setting. Bernard Maybeck is the unique architect in recent times to employ contradictory combinations of vernacular industrial elements and eclectic stylistic elements (for example, industrial sash and Gothic tracery) in the same building. Using convention unconventionally is otherwise almost unknown in our recent architecture.

Poets, according to Eliot, employ "that perpetual slight alteration of language, words perpetually juxtaposed in new and sudden combinations." [29] Wordsworth writes in his preface to the *Lyrical Ballads* of choosing "incidents and situations from common life [so that] ordinary things should be presented to the mind in an unusual aspect." [30] And Kenneth Burke has referred to "perspective by incongruity." [31] This technique, which seems basic to the medium of poetry, has been used today in another medium. The Pop painter gives uncommon meaning to common elements by changing their context or increasing their scale. Through "involvement in the relativity of perception and the relativity of meaning," [32] old clichés in new settings achieve rich meanings which are ambiguously both old and new, banal and vivid.

The value of such contradictory meanings has been acknowledged in both evolutionary and revolutionary architecture—from the collages of fragments of post-Roman architecture, the so-called Spolium architecture in which column capitals are used as bases, for instance, to the Renaissance style itself, where the old Classical Roman vocabulary was employed in new combinations. And James Ackerman has described Michelangelo as "rarely adopting a motif [in his architecture] without giving it a new form or a new meaning. Yet he invariably retained essential features from ancient models in order to force the observer to recollect the source while enjoying the innovations." [33]

Ironic convention is relevant both for the individual building and the townscape. It recognizes the real condition of our architecture and its status in our culture. Industry promotes expensive industrial and electronic research but not architectural experiments, and the Federal government diverts subsidies toward air transportation, communication, and the vast enterprises of war or, as they call it, national security, rather than toward the forces for the direct enhancement of life. The practicing architect must admit this. In simple terms, the budgets, techniques, and programs for his buildings must relate more to 1866 than 1966. Architects should accept their modest role rather than disguise it and risk what might be called an electronic expressionism, which might parallel the industrial expressionism of early Modern architecture. The architect who would accept his role as combiner of significant old clichés—valid banalities —in new contexts as his condition within a society that directs its best efforts, its big money, and its elegant technologies elsewhere, can ironically express in this indirect way a true concern for society's inverted scale of values.

I have alluded to the reasons why honky-tonk elements in our architecture and townscape are here to stay, especially in the important short-term view, and why such a fate should be acceptable. Pop Art has demonstrated that these commonplace elements are often the main source of the occasional variety and vitality of our cities, and that it is not their banality or vulgarity as elements which make for the banality or vulgarity of the whole scene, but rather their contextual relationships of space and scale.

Another significant implication from Pop Art involves method in city planning. Architects and planners who peevishly denounce the conventional townscape for its vulgarity or banality promote elaborate methods for abolishing or disguising honky-tonk elements in the existing landscape, or, for excluding them from the vocabulary of their new townscapes. But they largely fail either to enhance or to provide a substitute for the existing scene because they attempt the impossible. By attempting too much they flaunt their impotence and risk their continuing influence as supposed experts. Cannot the architect and planner, by slight adjustments to the conventional elements of the townscape, existing or proposed, promote significant effects? By modifying or adding conventional elements to still other conventional elements they can, by a twist of context, gain a maximum of effect through a minimum of means. They can make us see the same things in a different way.

Finally, standardization, like convention, can be another manifestation of the strong order. But unlike convention it has been accepted in Modern architecture as an enriching product of our technology, yet dreaded for its potential domination and brutality. But is it not standardization that is without circumstantial accommodation and without a creative use of context that is to be feared more than standardization itself? The ideas of order and circumstance, convention and context—of employing standardization in an unstandard way—apply to our continuing problem of standardization versus variety. Giedion has written of Aalto's unique "combination of standardization with irrationality so that standardization is no longer master but servant." [34] I prefer to think of Aalto's art as contradictory rather than irrational—an artful recognition of the circumstantial and the contextual and of the inevitable limits of the order of standardization.

7. Contradiction Adapted

The façades of two eighteenth century Neapolitan villas express two kinds, or two manifestations, of contradiction. In the Villa Pignatelli (62) the mouldings, which dip, become string courses and window heads at once. In the Villa Palomba (63) the windows, which disregard the bay system and puncture the exterior panels, are positioned by interior needs. The mouldings in the first villa adapt easily to their contradictory functions. The windows of the second villa clash violently with the panel configurations and pilaster rhythm: the inside order and the outside order are in an uncompromisingly contradictory relation.

In the first façade contradiction is adapted by accommodating and compromising its elements; in the second façade contradiction is juxtaposed by using contrasting superimposed or adjacent elements. Contradiction adapted is tolerant and pliable. It admits improvisation. It involves the disintegration of a prototype—and it ends in approximation and qualification. On the other hand, contradiction juxtaposed is unbending. It contains violent contrasts and uncompromising oppositions. Contradiction adapted ends in a whole which is perhaps impure. Contradiction juxtaposed ends in a whole which is perhaps unresolved.

These types of contradiction occur in the work of Le Corbusier. Contrasts in the plans of the Villa Savoye (5) and the Assembly Building in Chandigarh (64) correspond to those in the elevations of the Villa Pignatelli and the Villa Palomba. In the Villa Savoye the positions of some of the columns in the rectangular bay system adjust slightly to accommodate to particular spatial needs—one column is moved and another removed. In the Assembly Building although the grid of columns also adjusts to the exceptional plastic form of the assembly hall, in the juxtaposition of the hall itself and the grid, they do not adapt—the juxtaposition is violent and uncompromising not only in plan but also in sections, where it appears to have been thrust violently into the grid (65).

Kahn has said: "It is the role of design to adjust to the circumstantial." The interior rectangles of Palladio's palace plans are frequently distorted into nonrectangular configurations in order to adjust to the Vicenza street patterns. The resultant tensions give a vitality to the buildings not apparent in their ideal counterparts illustrated in the *Quattro Libri*. In the Palazzo Massimi (66) a curving rather than an angular distortion accommodated the façade to the street, which also curved before it was changed in the

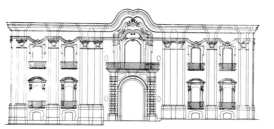

62. Villa Pignatelli, S. Giorgio a Cremano. Elevation

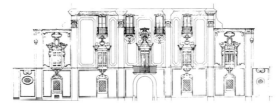

63. Villa Palomba, Torre del Greco. Elevation

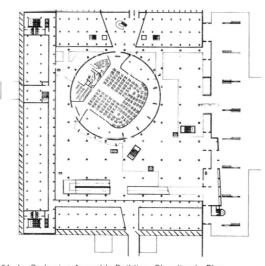

64. Le Corbusier. Assembly Building, Chandigarh. Plan

65. Le Corbusier. Assembly Building, Chandigarh. Section

66. Peruzzi. Palazzo Massimi, Rome

67. House, Domegge

nineteenth century. In the typical gambrel roof the need to accommodate living space within a roof angle essentially determined by drainage and structural functions results in an eloquent distortion of the original gable. These examples are distinguishable from the expressionistic distortions of Rococo or of German Expressionism where the distorted is not contrasted with the undistorted.

Besides circumstantial distortion, there are other techniques of adaptation. The expedient device is an element in all anonymous architecture that is dependent on a strong conventional order. It is used to adjust the order to circumstances which are contradictory to it: such circumstances are often topographical. The bracket on the house at Domegge (67) is a device that expedites the tense transition from symmetrical façade to symmetrical gable and at the same time accommodates the asymmetrical overhang on the right side. A vivid play of order and the circumstantial is, in fact, a characteristic of all Italian architecture, with its bold contradictions of monumentality and expediency. The ornamented post in the center of the inner portal at Vézelay (68), which is a shore for the lunette, interrupts the axis to the altar. It is an expedient device made eventful. Kahn's uniquely deep beams over the great span of the gymnasium in the project for the Trenton Community Center are exceptional devices to maintain the consistency of the domes of the roof. They are made manifest in plan by the filled-in-columns that support them (69). Lutyens' work abounds in devices: the split at the side of the house called The Salutation in Sandwich (70), is an expedient device which is spatial. By introducing natural illumination at the

68. Ste. Madeleine, Vézelay

46

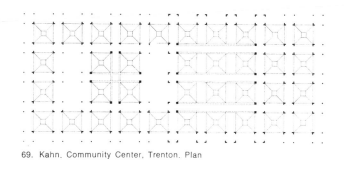

69. Kahn. Community Center, Trenton. Plan

70. Lutyens. The Salutation, Sandwich

71. Mount Vernon, Fairfax County, Va.

central stair landing, it breaks the order and promotes surprise in the classical prism of the house. (In some of Jasper Johns' painting the device is similarly made explicit by arrows and notation.)

Le Corbusier today is a master of the eventful exception, another technique of accommodation. He breaks the order of the bays in the ground floor of the Villa Savoye (5) by moving one column and removing another, as I have shown, to accommodate exceptional circumstances involving space and circulation. In this eloquent compromise Le Corbusier makes the dominant regularity of the composition more vivid.

The exceptional location of windows, like the eventful exception in columns, usually produces an altered symmetry. For example, the windows at Mount Vernon (71) do not follow an exact symmetrical pattern. Instead, the window pattern is the result of earlier renovations, and it breaks the dominant order of the central pediment and symmetrical wings. In McKim, Mead and White's Low House (72) the blatantly exceptional window positions in the north façade contradicted the consistent symmetrical

order of the outside shape to admit the circumstantial complexities of its domestic program. The very subtly distorted relationships of the windows in H. H. Richardson's house for Henry Adams in Washington (73) reflected the particular circumstances of the private functions inside, yet they maintained the regularity and symmetry demanded by the public function of a monumental building on Lafayette Square. Here the subtle compromise between order and circumstance, outside and inside, and private and public functions, produced ambiguous rhythms and vibrant tensions in the façade.

The varied openings in the Palazzo Tarugi (60), exceptional in form and position, break the dominant pilaster order of the outside in typical Italian fashion. Lewis Mumford, in a seminar at the University of Pennsylvania in 1963, compared the exceptional window positions in the south façade of the Doges' Palace with Eero Saarinen's windowed façade of the American Embassy in London. The dominant consistent rhythms in the Embassy building tend to deny the circumstantial complexities within its modern program and to express the dry purity of a civic bureauc-

72. McKim, Mead and White. Low House, Bristol, R.I.

73. Richardson. Adams House, Washington, D.C.

racy. The chapel wing at Versailles is an eventful exception beyond the scale of columns or windows. Through its position, form, and height it contributes a vitality and validity to the dominant symmetrical order of the whole, a vitality conspicuously lacking at Caserta, for example, where the exterior order of the enormous and complex palace is entirely consistent.

In Modern architecture we have operated too long under the restrictions of unbending rectangular forms supposed to have grown out of the technical requirements of the frame and the mass-produced curtain wall. In contrasting Mies' and Johnson's Seagram Building (74) with Kahn's project for an office tower in Philadelphia (75) it can be seen that Mies and Johnson reject all contradictions of diagonal wind-bracing in favor of an expression of a rectilinear frame. Kahn once said that the Seagram Building was like a beautiful lady with hidden corsets. Kahn, in contrast, expresses the wind-bracing—but at the expense of such vertical elements as the elevator and, indeed of the spaces for people.

In many works of Le Corbusier and Aalto, however, a balance, or perhaps a tension, is achieved between the rectilinearity of standard techniques, and the diagonal which expresses exceptional conditions. In his apartments at Bremen (76), Aalto has taken the rectangular order of Le Corbusier's basic dwelling unit, which makes up his high-rise apartment slabs (77), and distorted it into diagonals in order to orient the dwelling unit toward the south for light and for the view. The north-facing stairs and circulation areas remain strictly rectilinear in plan. Even in the most extreme units an essential rectilinearity and regularity of space is maintained. And in Aalto's Wolfsburg Cultural Center (78) the rectangular configuration of the whole composition is barely maintained as he organizes the necessarily diagonal shapes of the auditoriums.

This is different from Kahn's Goldenberg House project (79) where the exceptional diagonal is in part an element of the structural pattern and partially spatial, to make a series of spaces that go around the corners of the building continuously, rather than one side overlapping the other.

Mies allows nothing to get in the way of the consistency of his order, of the point, line, and plane of his always complete pavilions. If Wright camouflages his circumstantial exceptions, Mies excludes them: less is more. Since 1940 Mies has not used a circumstantial diagonal, and in

74. Mies van der Rohe and Johnson. Seagram Building, New York

75. Kahn. Project for an Office Tower, Philadelphia. Model

50

76. Aalto. Apartment Building, Bremen. Plan

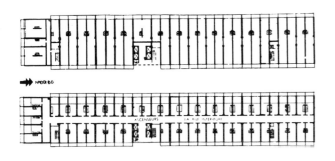

77. Le Corbusier. Apartment Building, Marseilles. Plan

79. Kahn. Project for the Goldenberg House. Plan

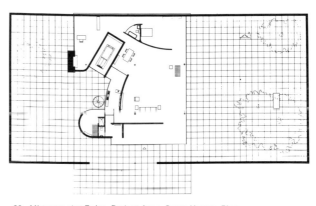

80. Mies van der Rohe. Project for a Court House. Plan

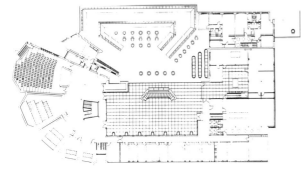

78. Aalto. Cultural Center, Wolfsburg. Plan

his series of courthouse projects of the 1930's (80) the diagonal is a function of the free plan rather than a condition of the circumstantial. Because the diagonal is dominant rather than exceptional and loosely contained in its rectangular frame, there is little tension between the diagonals and the rectangles. The diagonal chords of the trusses in Mies' large-span buildings are, of course, not circumstantial exceptions.

In the Villa Savoye, again, the exceptional diagonal of the ramp is clearly expedient in section and elevation (12) and allows Le Corbusier to create a strong opposition to the regular order of column bays and envelope. This attitude contrasts greatly with that of Wright, whose insistence on horizontal continuity at the expense of all else is well known. Even in the unusually exposed stair at Fallingwater (81) Wright suppresses all diagonals: there are no strings or railings, but only the horizontal planes of the treads and the vertical lines of the rods from which the stair is hung. Similarly, in the interior (82) Wright hides the stairs between walls (as he does in virtually all his houses), while Le Corbusier glories in the expressed diagonals of the ramp and the continuous diagonal of the spiral stair (5, 83). We have already seen how Le Corbusier accommodates architecture intimately to the exceptional needs of the automobile in the Villa Savoye (84). But Wright's order allows no inconsistencies: the bridge is perpendicular and analogous to the order of the house and the curving path of the automobile is not recognized. The driveway is like a path in the woods begrudgingly dotted in plan (82, 85). That the car can turn is almost fortuitous.

The diagonal, when suggested by circumstances inside or out, is seldom discordant. It hides within the order or else it dominates the composition as a motif. In the Vigo Schmidt House project the diagonal becomes part of the overall triangular module. In the David Wright House the whole building becomes a diagonal ramp. In the Guggenheim Museum, where the diagonal spiral is the dominant motival order in a more complex program, the rectangular perpendicular form does express exceptional circumstances. Inside, the vertical order of the structure, and particularly of the shaft containing toilets is expressed in order to provide stable measure for the converging spiral ramp.

Aalto, then, adapts the order to the circumstantial exception symbolized by the diagonal. So does Kahn in the examples given, although in the early schemes for the

81. Wright. Kaufmann House (Fallingwater), Bear Run, Pa.

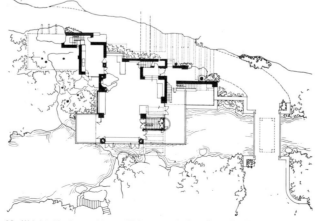

82. Wright. Kaufmann House (Fallingwater), Bear Run, Pa. Plan

83. Le Corbusier. Villa Savoye, Poissy

85. Wright. Kaufmann House (Fallingwater), Bear Run, Pa.

84. Le Corbusier. Villa Savoye, Poissy

capitol at Dacca an extreme rigidity predominates, despite the huge size and complexity of the project. Le Corbusier juxtaposes the exceptional diagonal. Mies excludes it. Wright hides it or surrenders his whole order to it: the exception becomes the rule.

These ideas are applicable to the design and perception of cities, which have more extensive and complex programs, of course, than individual buildings. The consistent spatial order of the Piazza S. Marco, for example (86), is not without its violent contradictions in scale, rhythm, and textures, not to mention the varying heights and styles of the surrounding buildings. Is there not a similar validity to the vitality of Times Square (87) in which the jarring inconsistencies of buildings and billboards are contained within the consistent order of the space itself? It is when honky-tonk spills out beyond spatial boundaries to the no-man's land of roadtown, that it becomes chaos and blight. (If in *God's Own Junkyard* Peter Blake had chosen examples of roadside landscape for his book which were less extremely "bad," his point, at least involving the banality of roadside architecture, would ironically have been stronger.) It seems our fate now to be faced with either the endless inconsistencies of roadtown (88), which is chaos, or the infinite consistency of Levittown (or the ubiquitous Levittown-like scene illustrated in figure 89), which is boredom. In roadtown we have a false complexity; in Levittown a false simplicity. One thing is clear—from such false consistency real cities will never grow. Cities, like architecture, are complex and contradictory.

86. Piazza S. Marco, Venice

87. Times Square, New York

88. Highway, U.S.A.

89. Developers' Houses, U.S.A.

The party moved on, but deviated a little from the straight way, in order to glance at the ponderous remains of the temple of Mars Ultor, within which a convent of nuns is now established,—a dove-cote, in the war-god's mansion. At only a little distance, they passed the portico of a Temple of Minerva, most rich and beautiful in architecture, but woefully gnawed by time and shattered by violence, besides being buried midway in the accumulation of soil, that rises over dead Rome like a floodtide. Within this edifice of an antique sanctity, a baker's shop was now established, with an entrance on one side; for, everywhere, the remnants of old grandeur and divinity have been made available for the meanest necessities of our day.*

90. Le Corbusier. Millowners' Building, Ahmedabad

If "contradiction adapted" corresponds to the kid glove treatment, "contradiction juxtaposed" involves the shock treatment. The Villa Pignatelli (62) *adapts variations,* but the Villa Palomba (63) *juxtaposes contrasts:* its contradictory relationships become manifest in discordant rhythms, directions, adjacencies, and especially in what I shall call superadjacencies—the superimpositions of various elements.

Le Corbusier supplies a rare modern example of juxtaposed contradictions in the Millowners' Building in Ahmedabad (90). From the important approach from the south, the repetitive pattern of the brise-soleil invokes rhythms which are violently broken by the entrance void, the ramp, and the stairs. These latter elements, consisting of varying diagonals, create violent adjacencies from the side and violent superadjacencies from the front, in relation to the rectangular static floor divisions within the boxlike form. The juxtapositions of diagonals and perpendiculars also create contradictory directions: the meeting of the ramp and stairs is only slightly softened by the exceptionally large void and by the modified rhythm of the elements at that part of the façade. But these contradictions in the visual experience are even richer when you move closer and penetrate the building. The adjacencies and superadjacencies of contrasting scales, directions, and functions can

* Nathaniel Hawthorne, *The Marble Faun,* Dell Publishing Co., Inc., New York, 1961.

91. Furness. Clearing House, Philadelphia

make it seem like a miniature example of Kahn's viaduct architecture. In Le Corbusier's Palace of the Two Assemblies at Chandigarh (65) the conical assembly hall jammed into the rectangular grid represents a more three-dimensional superadjacency of a very violent kind.

The city street façade can provide a type of juxtaposed contradiction that is essentially two-dimensional. Frank Furness' Clearing House (91), now demolished like many of his best works in Philadelphia, contained an array of violent pressures within a rigid frame. The half-segmental arch, blocked by the submerged tower which, in turn, bisects the façade into a near duality, and the violent adjacencies of rectangles, squares, lunettes, and diagonals of contrasting sizes, compose a building seemingly held up by the buildings next door: it is an almost insane short story of a castle on a city street. All these relationships of structure and pattern contradict the severe limitations associated with a façade, a street line, and contiguous row houses.

The rectangular face of the Palazzo del Popolo in Ascoli Piceno (92) illustrates juxtaposed contradiction that comes from repeated renovation rather than from the instantaneous stroke of a single architect. This façade teems with the violent adjacencies and superadjacencies of open and closed arcades, continuous and interrupted string courses, big and little windows, "porte" and "portone," and clocks, cartouches, balconies, and store fronts. All of these produce broken rhythms and reflect the contradictory dualities of public and private, ordered and circumstantial scales. The unflinching wings and striped patterns of Butterfield's All Saints Church, Margaret Street, London (93), clash when they come together. The relative independence of the form of the parts, despite their closeness, is a most significant example of contradiction juxtaposed as distinct from contradiction adapted.

It is the texture of Mannerist rustication which clashes in the same way when it abuts the precise detail of the classical orders in a Renaissance façade. But Michelangelo's loggia in the center of the upper floor of the rear façade of the Palazzo Farnese in relation to the walls adjacent to it reflects a more ambiguous kind of contradiction (94). Giacomo della Porta's exceptional central elements on the floor below—pilasters, arches and architrave—vary only slightly in rhythm and not at all in scale, and the transition from the typical window bays on each side to the middle bays is consistent in detail and scale. The openings of

92. Palazzo del Popolo, Ascoli Piceno

93. Butterfield. All Saints Church, Margaret Street, London

94. Michelangelo. Rear Façade, Palazzo Farnese, Rome

Michelangelo's loggia above are violently contrasting in scale and rhythm with the typical elements to the sides as well as in the higher floor elevation which they imply. The pilasters also, because of their elevation and height, violently break the frieze below the cornice; and the cornice itself recedes rather than advances to match the projections and boldness of the elements below it. The scale of this cornice is smaller because of the increased rhythm of the modillions, yet the modillions themselves (lions' heads) are identical to those on the other cornice and the mouldings are continuous throughout. Similarly ambiguous combinations of contradictions both juxtaposed and adapted, occur in the intermediate bays within the niche.

In Michelangelo's Medici Chapel in San Lorenzo (95) the almost furniture-like scale of ornament of the marble elements within the bays abuts the very big scale of the giant order of pilasters. Classical orders make for another kind of contrasting adjacency when the giant order is juxtaposed on the minor order and the proportion is constant regardless of size. Jefferson's combinations of column sizes at the University of Virginia (96) contradict the maxim that every magnitude requires its own structure. But the juxtapositions of elements contrasting in size yet proportional in shape, like the pyramids of Gizeh, characterize a primary technique of monumentality. In the cathedral façades at Granada (97) and Foligno (98) the adjacencies of varying-sized circles, semicircles, and triangles in the openings and pediments, and at Eastbury (99) Vanbrugh's giant arched openings, proportioned similarly to the arched windows upon which they are superimposed, create a strange tension not unlike that exploited in Jasper Johns' paintings of superimposed flags (100). The guest house which stood behind the Low House by McKim, Mead and White was a miniature imitation of that house in its distinctive overall form.

Besides these violent adajcencies there are contrasts of direction within the whole. The Church of the Holy Sepulchre in Jerusalem (101), much renovated, and Aalto's Cultural Center at Wolfsburg (78), pre-renovated, so to speak, contain walls and series of columns with contradictory directions of almost equal intensity. The wings and projections of the Shingle Style house called Kragsyde in Manchester-by-the-Sea (102) are less contained within a dominant perimeter, but nevertheless include a multiplicity of directions, especially in elevation.

95. Michelangelo. Medici Chapel. San Lorenzo, Florence

96. Jefferson. University of Virginia, Charlottesville

58

07. Granada Cathedral

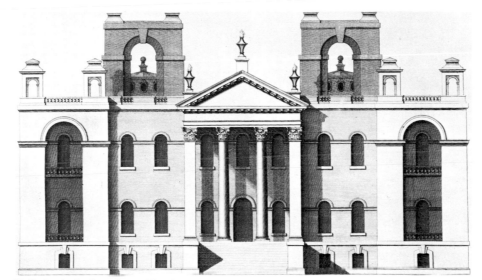

99. Vanbrugh. Eastbury, Dorset. Elevation

98. Foligno Cathedral

100. Johns. *Three Flags*. 1958

102. Peabody and Stearns. Black House (Kragsyde),
Manchester-by-the-Sea, Mass.

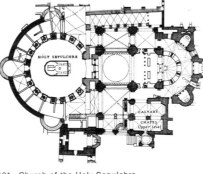

101. Church of the Holy Sepulchre,
Jerusalem. Plan

103. Empire-style Chair, Palazzo Reale, Caserta

104. Adler and Sullivan. Auditorium Building, Chicago

105. Anonymous Italian architecture

Juxtaposed directions create rhythmic complexities and contradictions. Figure 103 illustrates a chair at Caserta that contains violently contrasting curvilinear and rectangular rhythms. At another scale, the interior of Adler and Sullivan's Auditorium (104) has juxtapositions of swooping curves and diverse repetitions. In some anonymous Italian architecture (105) adjacent contrasting arcades contain contrapuntal rhythms.

Superadjacency is inclusive rather than exclusive. It can relate contrasting and otherwise irreconcilable elements; it can contain opposites within a whole; it can accommodate the valid non sequitur; and it can allow a multiplicity of levels of meaning, since it involves changing contexts—seeing familiar things in an unfamiliar way and from unexpected points of view. Superadjacency can be considered a variation of the idea of simultaneity expressed in Cubism and in certain orthodox Modern architecture, which employed transparency. But it is in contrast to the perpendicular interpenetration of space and form characteristic of the work of Wright. Superadjacency can result in a real richness as opposed to the surface richness of the screen which is typical of "serene" architecture. Its manifestations, as we shall see, are as diverse as Bramante's layered walls in the Belvedere Court in the Vatican Palace (106) and Kahn's "ruins . . . wrapped around buildings" in his Salk Institute for Biological Studies (107).

Superadjacency can exist between distant elements, such as the propylon before a Greek temple, which frames the composition and ties the foreground to the background. Such superimpositions change as one moves in space. Superadjacency can also occur where the superimposed elements actually touch instead of being related only visually. This is the method in Gothic and Renaissance architecture. The nave walls of Gothic cathedrals contain arcades of varying orders and scales. The shafts and ribs, band courses, and arches which make up these arcades penetrate and are superimposed upon each other. At Gloucester Cathedral (108) the superadjacency is contradictory in scale and direction: the enormous diagonal buttress crosses the plane of the delicate order of arcades in the transept's wall. All Mannerist and Baroque façades involve superadjacencies and interpenetrations on the same plane. Giant orders in relation to minor orders express contradictions in scale in the same building, and the series of superimposed pilasters in Baroque architecture implies spatial depth in a flat wall.

100. Bramante, Belvedere Court, Vatican, Rome

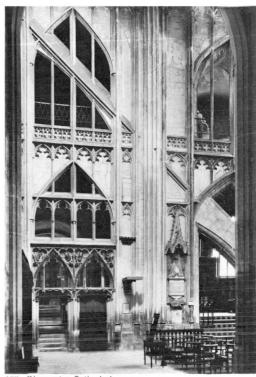

108. Gloucester Cathedral

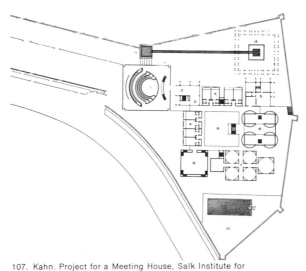

107. Kahn. Project for a Meeting House, Salk Institute for Biological Studies, La Jolla. Plan

Vignola's sculptural superimposition of portal and portico in his pavilion at Bomarzo (17) and the amputated pilasters of the entrance facade of the Belén church in Cuzco are perhaps intriguing solecisms, but the complex superadjacencies in the cloister façades at Tomar (109) compose a wall validly containing spaces within itself. The multiple layers of columns—engaged and disengaged, large and small, directly and indirectly superimposed—and the profusion of superimposed openings, architraves, and horizontal and diagonal balustrades create contrasts and contradictions in scale, direction, size, and shape. They make a wall containing spaces inside itself. I shall return to this kind of valid redundancy in the next chapter concerning the difference between the inside and the outside.

The diverse structural elements that surround the great door in the Porta Pia (110, 111) are superimposed for ornament as well as structure. It abounds in redundant and rhetorical superadjacencies of a kind of ornament that is "about" structure. The vulnerable edges of the opening are protected by rusticated trim at the sides. Superimposed on the trim are pilasters that further define the sides of the door and support, together with the scrolled brackets above, the heavy complex of the pediment. This important opening is made eventful in the bearing wall by additional juxtapositions. The diagonal pediment protects the rectangular inscription block and the inverse segment of the sculptural garland which, in turn, plays against the curve of the semicircular relieving arch. The arch is at the head of a series of redundant structural spanning elements, including the horizontal lintel, which in turn relieves the flat arch, which is a continuation of the rusticated trim. Brackets or corbeling, which decrease the span, are suggested by the diagonals of the top corners of the opening. The exaggerated keystone is superimposed on the flat-arch, the lintel, and the tympanum of the arch.

In their complex relationships these elements are in varying degrees both structural and ornamental, frequently redundant, and sometimes vestigial. In the almost equal combination of horizontal, vertical, diagonal, and curve they correspond to Sullivan's violently superimposed frames around the bull's-eye window of the boxlike Merchants' National Bank in Grinnell, Iowa (112).

In Lutyens' project for Liverpool Cathedral (113) the scattered minute windows seen as black dots impose themselves in an independent pattern on the symmetrical, monu-

109. Arruda. Convent of Christ, Tomar, Portugal

110. Michelangelo. Porta Pia, Rome

111. Michelangelo. Porta Pia, Rome

112. Sullivan. Merchants' National Bank, Grinnell, Iowa

113. Lutyens. Project for Liverpool Cathedral. Model

mental forms of the whole building. The pliable pattern of little windows accommodates service areas required for upkeep of the building and creates human scale that contrasts with the rigid monumentality. In Philadelphia the gridiron street pattern of the local scale of circulation is superimposed upon the resultant diagonal avenues which correspond to the regional scale of circulation in the city because they originally connected the center with the outlying towns. These juxtapositions create unique, residual, triangular blocks containing unusually shaped buildings, which give the city visual variety and quality. The "squares" in Manhattan formed by the unique diagonal intersections of Broadway—for instance, Madison, Union, Herald, and Times Squares—became events each with its individual character, which added vitality and tension to the overall gridiron of that city. The almost inevitable contradictory diagonal of the railroad tracks in the typical American gridiron town of the plains also vividly implies the contrasting scale of the whole region. The nineteeenth century American "elevated" which was juxtaposed above the street anticipated the multi-level city like Sigmond's 1958 plan for Berlin (114) which proposed a multi-level city with large-scale circulation elevated above the local traffic. In this kind of superimposition the degree of separation lies between the changing, almost incidental superimpositions of forms that are very separate in space and the interpenetration of superimpositions on the same plane. Superadjacencies at this intermediate degree are closely related but not touching, like the configuration of a separated lining. They are also rare in Modern architecture.

The Romanesque arcades on the cathedral at Lucca (115), the Gothic traceries of the cathedral at Strasbourg (116), or the interior of the choir at Notre Dame, Paris (117), the Renaissance galleries at Chambord (118), or the outside second floor colonnettes of Gaudí's Casa Battló (119), or the columns in the gallery inside his Casa Güell (120), are all disengaged and superimposed on contrasting window patterns. The big public-scale and the rigid order outside contrast vividly with the small private-scale patterns required within. This play of layers of openings is sometimes discordant in rhythm and scale: Vanbrugh's giant arched opening at Eastbury (99) and Armando Brazini's in the Forestry Building at the E.U.R. site in Rome (121) illustrated the same kind of superadjacency on the inner and outer walls, but Brazini's was rhythmically discordant.

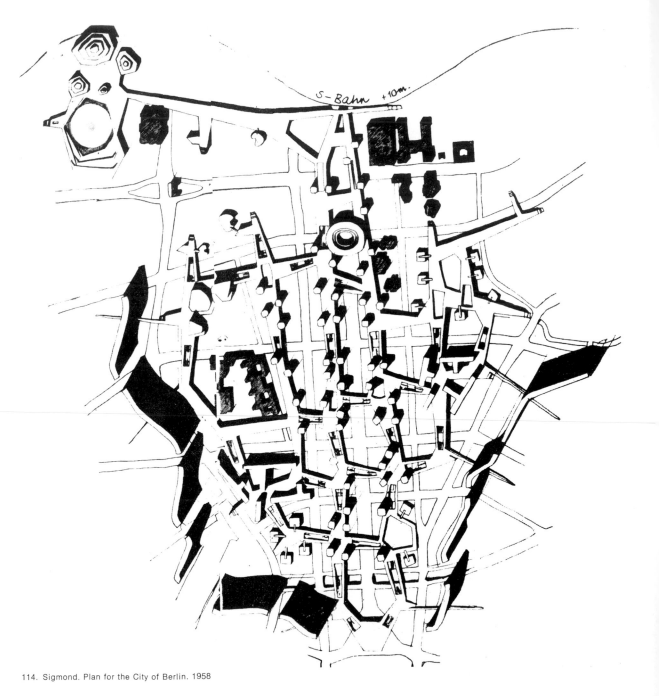

114. Sigmond. Plan for the City of Berlin. 1958

115. Lucca Cathedral

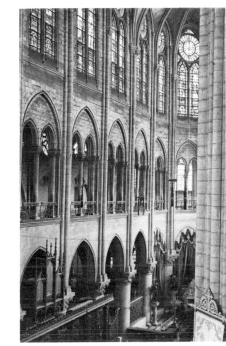

117. Notre Dame, Paris

119. Gaudí. Casa Battló, Barcelona

116. Strasbourg Cathedral

118. Nepveu. Château, Chambord

120. Gaudí. Casa Güell, Barcelona

On Vanbrugh's entrance facade to the kitchen court at Blenheim (59), disengaged columns, which frame the grand opening, are discordantly superimposed upon the windows that make up part of the regular rhythmic pattern behind. The same thing happens at Seaton Delaval (122), where the disengaged columns block some of the windows. The façade of St. Maclou, Rouen (123), is made up of layers of diagonal elements—traceried pediments, roofs, and buttresses—differing in function though analogous in form. These juxtapositions are relatively separated in comparison with the façade of Il Redentore (51), whose ambiguously superimposed diagonals are broken pediments and exposed buttresses at the same time.

Other buildings contain similar degrees of spatial superadjacencies on the inside taking the form of extremely articulated or separated linings. In the choir of the Wieskirche (124) the colonnade, which runs closely parallel to the walls, makes changing rhythmic juxtapositions against the pilasters and window openings of the walls. Soane's interior arch in the Insolvent Debtors' Court, London (125), makes a more contradictory superadjacency against the windows of the wall almost immediately beyond.

In Modern architecture contradictory juxtapositions of scale involving immediately adjacent elements are even rarer than superadjacencies. Such a manipulation of scale is seen in the accidental collage of the colossal head of Constantine and the louvered shutters in the courtyard of the Capitoline Museum (126). Significantly, it is usually in non-architectural configurations (127) that such contrasts in scale occur today. In another context I have referred to the adjacencies of giant and minor orders in Mannerist and Baroque architecture. In the rear façade of St. Peter's (128, 129) Michelangelo makes an even more contradictory contrast in scale: a blank window is juxtaposed with a capital bigger than the window itself. In the cathedral façade at Cremona (130) there is a violent adjacency of little arcades and an enormous rose window high up. This reflects within the building both the scale of the building itself and the scale of the town it dominates so that the building accommodates the close view and yet commands from a distance. In the cathedral at Cefalù (131) the symbolically important mosaic figure of Christ is correspondingly big in relation to the other ornament. The enormous central door, which is equal to the giant scale of the columns of the portico of the Temple of Apollo at Didyma (132), con-

121. Brazini. Forestry Building, E.U.R., Rome

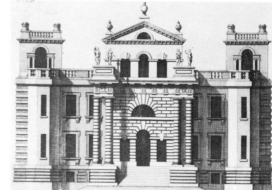

122. Vanbrugh. Seaton Delaval, Northumberland. Elevation

123. St. Maclou, Rouen

124. Zimmerman. Wieskirche, Steingaden, Bavaria

125. Soane. Insolvent Debtors' Court, London

126. Court, Capitoline Museum,
Rome

127. Smokestack, Cunard Line

128. Michelangelo. Rear Facade,
St. Peter's, Rome

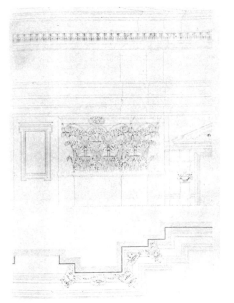

129. Michelangelo. Rear Façade, St. Peter's, Rome.
Ornament design

130. Cremona Cathedral

131. Cefalù Cathedral, Sicily

trasts with the little side doors of the same façade. Like Lutyens at Middleton Park (133), Le Corbusier in the Villa Stein (134) contrasts the scale of the entrance and service doors. This contrast is intensely vivid, not because they are adjacent, but because the doors have equivalent positions in an essentially symmetrical façade. In the Casa Güell (135) Gaudí superimposes the large door for vehicles and the little door for pedestrians. A vivid tension evolves from all these juxtaposed contradictions. Sometimes close changes of scale are encountered in our cities. but these usually occur more through accidents than design, like the vestigial Trinity Church on Wall Street or some juxtapositions of expressways and existing buildings (136), which are perversions of the hyperproximities of little houses and grand cathedrals or city walls in medieval cities. Some city planners, however, are now more prone to question the glibness of orthodox zoning and to allow violent proximities in their planning, at least in theory, than are architects within their buildings.

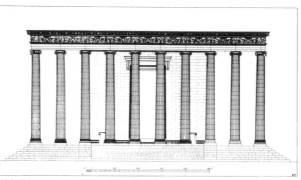

132. Temple of Apollo, Didyma. Elevation

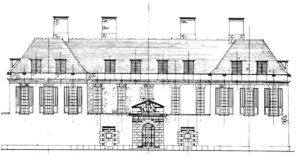

133. Lutyens. Middleton Park, Oxfordshire. Elevation

134. Le Corbusier. Villa Stein, Garches

135. Gaudí. Casa Güell, Barcelona

136. Expressways, California

The external configuration is usually rather simple, but there is packed into the interior of an organism an amazing complexity of structures which have long been the delight of anatomists.

The specific form of a plant or animal is determined not only by the genes in the organism and the cytoplasmic activities that these direct but by the interaction between genetic constitution and environment. A given gene does not control a specific trait, but a specific reaction to a specific environment.*

Contrast between the inside and the outside can be a major manifestation of contradiction in architecture. However, one of the powerful twentieth century orthodoxies has been the necessity for continuity between them: the inside should be expressed on the outside. But this is not really new—only our means have been new. The Renaissance church interior, for instance (137), has a continuity with its exterior; the interior vocabulary of pilasters, cornices, and drip mouldings is almost identical in scale and sometimes in material with its exterior vocabulary. The result is subtle modification but little contrast and no surprise.

Perhaps the boldest contribution of orthodox Modern architecture was its so-called flowing space, which was used to achieve the continuity of inside and outside. The idea has been emphasized by historians ranging from Vincent Scully's discovery of its early evolution in Shingle Style interiors to its flowering in the Prairie House and its culmination in De Stijl and the Barcelona Pavilion. Flowing space produced an architecture of related horizontal and vertical planes. The visual independence of these uninterrupted planes was scored by connecting areas of plate glass: windows as holes in the wall disappeared and became, instead, interruptions of wall to be discounted by the eye as a positive element of the building. Such cornerless architecture implied an ultimate continuity of space. Its emphasis on the oneness of interior and exterior space was permitted by new mechanical equipment which for the first time made the inside thermally independent of the outside.

* Edmund W. Sinnott, *The Problem of Organic Form,* Yale University Press, New Haven, 1963.

But the old tradition of enclosed and contrasted inside space, which I want to analyze here, has been recognized by some Modern masters, even if it has not been much emphasized by the historians. Although Wright did in fact "destroy the box" in the Prairie House, the rounded corners and solid walls of the Johnson Wax Administration Building are analogous to the diagonal and rounded corners of Borromini's interiors and those of his eighteenth century followers—and for the same purpose: to exaggerate a sense of horizontal enclosure and to promote the separateness and unity of the interior space by the continuity of the four walls. But Wright, unlike Borromini, did not puncture his continuous walls with windows. That would have weakened the bold contrast of horizontal enclosure and vertical openness. And it also would have been too traditional and structurally ambiguous for him.

The essential purpose of the interiors of buildings is to enclose rather than direct space, and to separate the inside from the outside. Kahn has said: "A building is a harboring thing." The function of the house to protect and provide privacy, psychological as well as physical, is an ancient one. The Johnson Wax Building fosters a further tradition: the expressive differentiation of the inside and outside spaces. Besides enclosing the inside with walls, Wright differentiated the interior light, an idea with a rich evolution from Byzantine, Gothic, and Baroque architecture to that of Le Corbusier and Kahn today. The inside *is* different from the outside.

But there are other valid means of differentiating and relating inside and outside space which are foreign to our recent architecture. Eliel Saarinen said that just as a building is the "organization of space in space. So is the community. So is the city." [35] I think this series could start with the idea of a room as a space in space. And I should like to apply Saarinen's definition of relationships not only to the spatial relationships of building and site, but to those of interior spaces within interior spaces. What I am talking about is the baldacchino above the altar and within the sanctuary. Another classic building of Modern architecture, again admittedly not typical, illustrates my point. The Villa Savoye (12) with its wall openings which are, significantly, holes rather than interruptions, restricts any flowing space rigidly to the vertical direction. But there is a spatial implication beyond that of enclosure which contrasts it with the Johnson Wax Building. Its severe, almost square exterior

137. Martini. Church of the Madonna del Calcinaio, Cortona

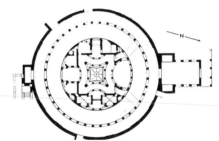

138. Maritime Theatre, Hadrian's Villa, Tivoli. Plan

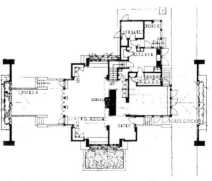

139. Wright. Evans House, Chicago. Plan

surrounds an intricate interior configuration glimpsed through openings and from protrusions above. In this context the tense image of the Villa Savoye from within and without displays a contrapuntal resolution of severe envelope partly broken and intricate interior partly revealed. Its inside order accommodates the multiple functions of a house, domestic scale, and partial mystery inherent in a sense of privacy. Its outside order expresses the unity of the idea of house at an easy scale appropriate to the green field it dominated and possibly to the city it will one day be part of.

A building can include things within things as well as spaces within spaces. And its interior configurations can contrast with its container in other ways besides those of the Villa Savoye's. The circular perimeters of bearing wall and colonnade in Hadrian's Maritime Theatre at Tivoli (138) produce another version of the same spatial idea. Even Wright, although only by suggestion, contains the interior intricacy of his Evans House (139) with a rectangular envelope implied by the sculptural corner posts. At the other extreme, the intricacies within the plan of the typical Tudor manor, Barrington Court (13), for example, are hidden, maybe excessively and expressed only incidentally, if at all, on its rigid, symmetrical façades. In another symmetrical Tudor plan the kitchen balances the chapel. The intricacies revealed in section in the château at Marly (140, 141) are a concession to light and convenience inside. Because they are not expressed on the outside, the interior light is surprising. Fuga's walls wrap around S. Maria Maggiore (142), and Soane's walls enclose the distorted intricacies of courtyards and wings of the Bank of England (143) in the same way and for similar reasons: they unify outside, in relation to the scale of the city, the contradictory spatial intricacies of chapels or banking rooms which evolved in time. Crowded intricacies can be excluded as well as contained. The colonnades at St. Peter's (144) and at the Piazza del Plebiscito in Naples (145), respectively exclude the intricacies of the Vatican Palace complex and the city complex, in order to achieve unity for their piazzas.

Sometimes the contradiction is not between the inside and the outside but between the top and the bottom of the building. The curving dome and drum on pendentives in Baroque churches protrude beyond the parapets of their rectangular bases. I have already mentioned in the P.S.F.S. skyscraper the curved base, rectangular shaft, and angled

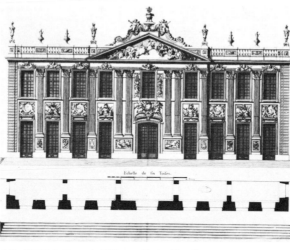

140. Hardouin-Mansart. Château, Marly. Elevation

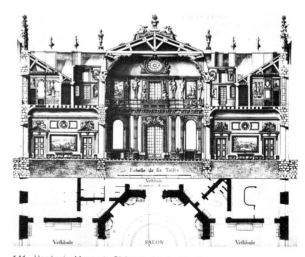

141. Hardouin-Mansart. Château, Marly. Section

142. S. Maria Maggiore, Rome

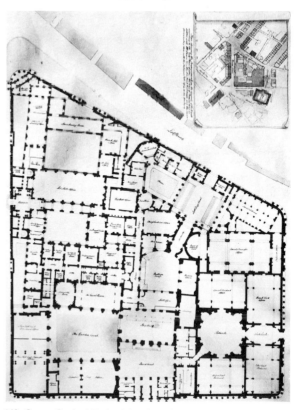

143. Soane. Bank of England, London. Plan

71

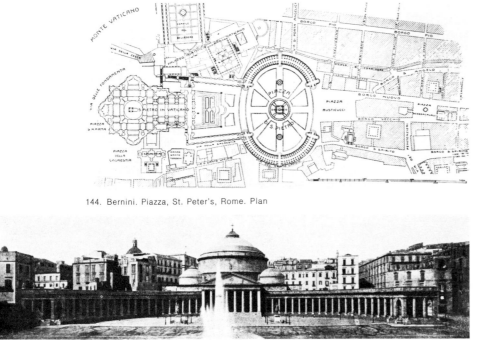

144. Bernini. Piazza, St. Peter's, Rome. Plan

145. Piazza del Plebiscito, Naples

146. Piranesi. Castel Sant' Angelo, Rome. *Vedute di Roma*

top as manifestations of multiple functions contained within the building (41). In the Castel Sant' Angelo (146) the rectangular elements evolve from a circular base. The Romantic roof-scapes of Richardson's Watts-Sherman House (147) and the multidomed trulli of Puglia (148) contrast with the severe exterior perimeters of their lower walls. From the outside, the space within a space can become the thing behind a thing. The enormous clerestory of Wollaton Hall (149) reads as a big-scale thing behind a smaller-scale thing. In S. Maria della Pace (150) the superimposition of enclosing elements, which are successively convex, perpendicular, and then concave, become contrasting things behind things to work transitions between the outside and the inside.

Essentially, Le Corbusier's plan of the Villa Savoye exemplifies crowded intricacies within a rigid frame. Some of the plans of his other houses of the '20's suggest starting with the frame and then working inward. Similar things happen in elevation in his High Court Building at Chandigarh (151). Like the rear of McKim, Mead and White's Low House (72), but at another scale, it contains intricacies within a rigid façade. The severe roof and wall envelope of the house contain complex spaces and floor levels which are expressed by varying window positions. Similarly, the single, sheltering gable of the Emmental-type house in Switzerland (152), and the constant shed of Aalto's Maison Carrée (153), contradict the interior spaces below. And similar tensions in the rear façade of Mt. Vernon (71) result from the contrast of the severe pedimented envelope and the irregular window positions. In the side façade of Hawksmoor's Easton Neston (154), the windows are positioned by particular interior requirements in defiance of its horizontal order. Crowded intricacy within a rigid frame has been a pervasive idea. It exists in such diverse examples as a fantasy of Piranesi (155) and the composition of a Michelangelo niche (156). More purely expressive examples are the façades of the parish church in Lampa, Peru (157), and the chapel entrance in Fontainebleau (158), which contain enormous pressures within their borders like a Mannerist painting.

147. Richardson. Watts-Sherman House, Newport

148. Trulli, Puglia, Italy

149. Smithson. Wollaton Hall, Nottinghamshire

150. Cortona. S. Maria della Pace, Rome

151. Le Corbusier. High Court Building, Chandigarh

152. Emmental-type House, Switzerland

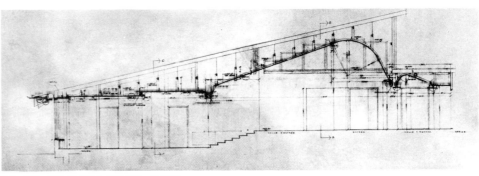

153. Aalto. Maison Carré, Bazoches. Section

154. Hawksmoor. Easton Neston, Northamptonshire

155. Piranesi. Ancient Baths. *Opere Varie*

Containment and intricacy have been characteristic of the city as well. Fortified walls for military protection and the greenbelt for civic protection are examples of this phenomenon. Contained intricacy might be one of the viable methods for dealing with urban chaos and the endlessness of roadtown; through the creative use of zoning and positive architectural features it is possible to concentrate the intricacies of roadtowns and junkyards, actual and figurative. And like the sculpture which consists of compressed automobiles by John Chamberlain and the photographs through telescopic lens in Blake's *God's Own Junkyard*, they achieve an ironically compelling kind of unity.

Contradiction between the inside and the outside may manifest itself in an unattached lining which produces an additional space between the lining and the exterior wall. Plan diagrams (159) illustrate that such layers between the inside space and the outside space can be more or less contrasting in shape, position, pattern, and size. Diagram 159a illustrates the simplest kind which is analogous and attached. A different material inside, wainscoting in this case, provides the contrast. The Byzantine mosaics inside the chapel of Galla Placidia represent a lining attached but contrasting in richness of texture, pattern, and color with the drab brickwork of the exterior. The pilasters, architraves, and arches of Renaissance walls, such as Bramante's façade in the Belvedere Court in the Vatican, can imply layers while the colonnade of the loggia of the south façade of the Louvre makes spatial layers. The colonnettes in the interior of the cathedral at Rouen (160) or the disengaged pilasters in the anteroom of Syon House (161) represent more detached kinds of layers also, but their subtle contrast to the outside depends more on scale than on form and texture. The lining becomes semidetached in Percier and Fontaine's curtained bedroom at Malmaison, which is derived from a Roman military tent. The graduated series of symbolic doors at Karnak (162) are multiple linings in relief similar in two dimensions to the generic idea of nests of toy eggs or wooden dolls. These doors within doors, like the multi-framed doors in Gothic porches, differ from multi-pedimented Baroque openings, which juxtapose triangular and segmental shapes.

The graduated series of things in things or enclosures within enclosures which characterize the Egyptian temple carry out in space the motif of the multi-framed doors at Karnak. The series of walls at Edfu (163, 164) are de-

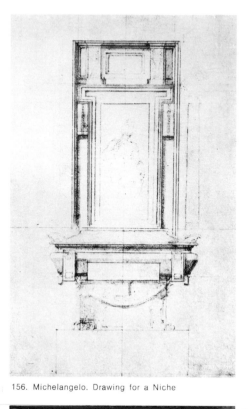

156. Michelangelo. Drawing for a Niche

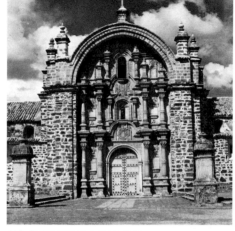

157. Parish Church, Lampa, Peru

158. Rosso and Primaticcio. Chapel Entrance, Fontainebleau

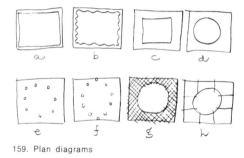

159. Plan diagrams

160. Rouen Cathedral

161. Adam. Syon House, Isleworth, Middlesex

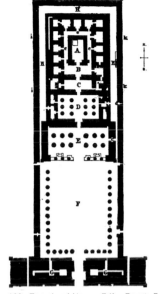

163. Temple of Horus, Edfu, Egypt. Plan

162. Doors, Karnak, Egypt

164. Temple of Horus, Edfu, Egypt

165. Bernini. S. Maria dell' Assunzione, Arricia

166. Albi Cathedral

167. Asam Brothers. Project. Elevation and section

168. Asam Brothers. Abbey Church, Weltenburg

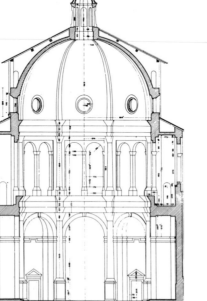

169. S. Maria in Canepanova, Pavia. Section

170. Rosati and Soria. S. Carlo ai Catinari, Rome

171. Soane. Soane House and Museum, Lincoln's Inn Fields, London

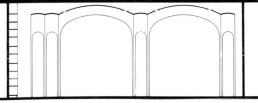

172, 173. Brazini. Church of the Cuore Immaculata di Maria Santissima, Rome

174. Johnson. Guest House, New Canaan. Section

tached linings. The outer linings enhance the enclosed inner spaces by making them seem protected and mysterious. They resemble the layers of fortifications in medieval castles, or the spatial nest in which Bernini contained his little Pantheon, S. Maria dell' Assunzione at Arricia (165). The same tensions occur between the hovering layers of the enclosing sanctuary screens and the outer walls of the cathedral at Albi (166) and other cathedrals in Catalonia and the Languedoc. The multiple domes of the Baroque represent, in section, layers which are analogous but detached. Through their central oculi one can see spaces beyond spaces. In the project by the Asam Brothers (167), for instance, the inner dome with its oculus masks high windows, thus producing surprising effects of light and a more complex space. On the exterior the upper dome increases the effect of scale and height. In their Abbey church at Weltenburg (168) the clouds of the frescoed upper dome, which are viewed through the oculus of the lower dome, increase the sense of space. In S. Maria in Canepanova in Pavia (169) the effect of the layered dome is seen on the outside rather than the inside.

The multiple domes of the S. Cecilia Chapel in S. Carlo ai Catinari in Rome (170) are detached and con-

trasting in shape. Beyond the oval oculus of the lower dome is seen a rectangular space flooded with light, containing a sculptural quartet of musical angels. Beyond this zone, in turn, floats an even more brilliant oval lantern. Soane uses interior domes in square spaces even in small areas like the breakfast room at Lincoln's Inn Fields (171). His fantastic juxtapositions of domes and lanterns, squinches and pendentives, and a variety of other ornamental and structural shapes elsewhere (35) work to enrich the sense of enclosure and light. These layered structural-ornamental elements are sometimes vestigial (almost in a two dimensional pattern), but they give the complex effect of actually detached spatial layers. Armando Brazini's neo-Baroque church of the Cuore Immaculata di Maria Santissima in Rome (172, 173) has a quasi-circular plan containing a Greek cross plan. The Greek cross plan is reflected on the outside in four pedimented porches marking the ends of the cross. These porches, in turn, are made convex to accommodate to the circular plan. In Modern architecture Johnson has been almost unique in emphasizing multiple enclosure in plan and section. The canopy inside his guest house in New Canaan (174) and the Soanian canopy within the synagogue in Port Chester (175) are both inner

175. Johnson. Kneses Tifereth Israel Synagogue, Port Chester, N.Y.

layers. Kahn employs detached layers on the outside: he "wraps ruins around buildings." In the project for the Meeting House for the Salk Institute for Biological Studies (107) he juxtaposes in plan circles within squares, and squares within circles. According to Kahn, inside glare will be counteracted by the juxtaposition of apertures, contrasting in size and shape, in the double-layered walls. Kahn has talked of the modification of light more than the spatial expression of enclosure as his reason for the contrasting layers. Lutyens' motif of the circle in the square appears in his stairs with round wells within square rooms.

In the vestibule of S. Croce in Gerusalemme (176) and in the interiors of SS. Sergius and Bacchus (177) and of St. Stephen Walbrook (34) it is the series of columns which define the inner, detached and contrasting layer of enclosure. These supports, along with the domes above them, make the intraspatial relationships of the interior. St. Stephen Walbrook is a square space containing an octagonal space at the lower level (178). Its squinch-like arches, at the intermediate level between the columns and the dome, make a transition to the dome above. Similarly, in Vierzehnheiligen (31) the piers along with the domes define curving spaces within the rectangular and hexagonal walls of the perimeter. But the inner layers are less independent than those in St. Stephen. In plan as well as section, the curve sometimes touches the outer wall and becomes common with it (179). Both the plan and section of Neresheim in Southern Germany (180) show that the complex curves of the inner circle sinuously inflect as they near the outer oval. These intraspatial relationships are at once more complex and more ambiguous than those of St. Stephen Walbrook's.

Layers are implied in Michelangelo's Sforza Chapel in S. Maria Maggiore (181, 182) in the violent penetrations of rectangular space and curved space in plan and of barrel vaults, domes and niche-vaulting in section. The ambiguous juxtapositions of these two kinds of shapes as well as the implied intense compression and enormous scale of the flatly curved spaces (which by implication extend beyond the actual enclosure) give this interior its peculiar power and tension (183).

Detached linings leave spaces in between. But the architectural recognition of the in-between varies. Edfu is almost all layers. The residual spaces are closed and dominate the small space at the center. St. Basel's (184) is like a

176. Gregorini and Passalacqua. S. Croce in Gerusalemme, Rome

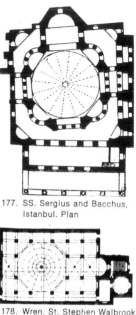

177. SS. Sergius and Bacchus, Istanbul. Plan

178. Wren. St. Stephen Walbrook, London. Plan

179. Neumann. Pilgrimage Church, Vierzehnheiligen, near Banz

180. Neumann. Abbey Church, Neresheim, W. Germany

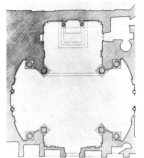

181. Michelangelo. Sforza Chapel, S. Maria Maggiore, Rome. Plan

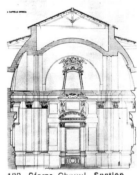

182. Sforza Chapel, Section

183. Sforza Chapel

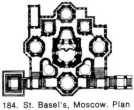

184. St. Basel's, Moscow. Plan

79

series of churches within a church. The intricate maze of residual spaces inside results from the proximity of the chapels to each other toward the center, and the closeness of the wrapping wall toward the outside. In Charles V's palace at Granada (185), the Villa Farnese at Caprarola (186), and the Villa Giulia (187), the courtyards dominate because they are large and their shapes contrast with the shape of the perimeters. They make the primary space; the rooms of the palaces are leftover space. As in the preliminary scheme of Kahn's Unitarian Church in Rochester (188), the residual spaces are closed. In contrast, the linings of columns and piers in SS. Sergius and Bacchus, St. Stephen Walbrook, Vierzehnheiligen, and Neresheim define residual spaces which open on the dominant spaces, although they are separate from them in varying degrees. In the Stupinigi Palace (189) because the dominant space is so open, the distinction between dominant and residual spaces in the main hall is ambiguous. In fact, the inner lining is so open that there remains only a vestige of a central inner space, indicated by four piers and the very complex vaulting patterns of the ceiling. The complex oculus and other openings of the inner dome in S. Chiara, Brà (190, 191), define residual space, which is open in order to elaborate space and manipulate light. The detachment of the inner and outer window openings in Aalto's Imatra Church (192) similarly modifies light and space. The use of this method is unique in recent architecture.

The wooden vaulting of seventeenth century Polish synagogues (193), which imitates masonry, makes closed linings in the upper section. In contrast to the previous examples their residual space is closed. Closed poché determined primarily by exterior spatial forces rather than the inherent structure of the form is almost unknown in Modern architecture except for Aalto's unique Concert Podium (194) composed of a wood skin-frame structure, which directs sound as well as space. Residual space in between dominant spaces with varying degrees of openness can occur at the scale of the city and is a characteristic of the fora and other complexes of late Roman urban planning. Residual spaces are not unknown in our cities. I am thinking of the open spaces under our highways and the buffer spaces around them. Instead of acknowledging and exploiting these characteristic kinds of space we make them into parking lots or feeble patches of grass—no-man's lands between the scale of the region and the locality.

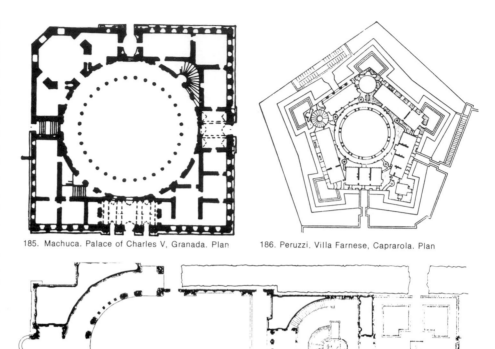

185. Machuca. Palace of Charles V, Granada. Plan

186. Peruzzi. Villa Farnese, Caprarola. Plan

187. Vignola. Villa Giulia, Rome. Plan

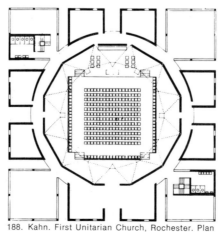

188. Kahn. First Unitarian Church, Rochester. Plan

189. Juvarra. Stupinigi Palace, near Turin

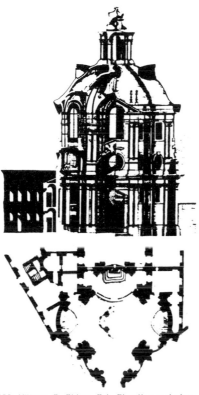

190. Vittone. S. Chiara, Brà. Elevation and plan

191. Vittone. S. Chiara, Brà

192. Aalto. Church, Vuoksenniska, near Imatra

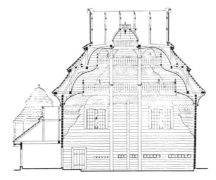

193. Polish Synagogue, 17th Century. Elevation

194. Aalto. Concert Podium, Turku

Residual space that is open might be called "open poché." Kahn's "servant space," which sometimes harbors mechanical equipment, and the poché in the walls of Roman and Baroque architecture are alternative means of accommodating an inside different from the outside. Aldo van Eyck has said: "Architecture should be conceived of as a configuration of intermediary places clearly defined. This does not imply continual transition or endless postponement with respect to place and occasion. On the contrary, it implies a break away from the contemporary concept (call it sickness) of spatial continuity and the tendency to erase every articulation between spaces, i.e., between outside and inside, between one space and another (between one reality and another). Instead the transition must be articulated by means of defined in-between places which induce simultaneous awareness of what is significant on either side. An in-between space in this sense provides the common ground where conflicting polarities can again become twin phenomena." [36]

Residual space is sometimes awkward. Like structural poché it is seldom economic. It is always leftover, inflected toward something more important beyond itself. The qualifications, contrasts, and tensions inherent in these spaces are perhaps cogent to Kahn's statement that "a building should have bad spaces as well as good spaces."

Redundant enclosure, like crowded intricacies, is rare in our architecture. With some significant exceptions in the work of Le Corbusier and Kahn, Modern architecture has tended to ignore such complex spatial ideas. The "utility core" of Mies or early Johnson is not relevant because it becomes a passive accent in a dominant open space, rather than an active parallel to another perimeter. Contradictory interior space does not admit Modern architecture's requirement of a unity and continuity of all spaces. Nor do layers in depth, especially with contrapuntal juxtapositions, satisfy its requirements of economic and unequivocal relationships of forms and materials. And crowded intricacy within a rigid boundary (which is not a transparent framework) contradicts the modern tenet which says that a building grows from the inside out.

What are the justifications for multiple enclosure and for the inside's being different from the outside? When Wright expressed his dictum: "an organic form grows its structure out of conditions as a plant grows out of the soil, both unfold similarly from within," [37] he had a long prece-

dent behind him. Other Americans had advocated what was at the moment a healthy thing—a needed battle cry:

> Greenough: Instead of forcing the functions of every sort of building into one general form, adopting an outward shape for the sake of the eyes or association, without references to the inner distribution, let us begin from the heart as a nucleus and work outward. [38]

> Thoreau: What of architectural beauty I now see, I know has grown gradually from within outward, out of the necessities and character of the indweller. [39]

> Sullivan: [The architect] must cause a building to grow naturally, logically, and poetically out of its condition. [40] . . . Outward appearances resemble inner purposes. [41]

Even Le Corbusier has written: "The plan proceeds from within to without; the exterior is the result of an interior." [42]

But Wright's biological analogy is self-limiting, because the development of a plant is influenced into particular distortions by the particular forces of its environment as well as by its genetic order of growth. D'Arcy Wentworth Thompson saw form as a record of development in environment. The inherently rectangular order of structure and space of Aalto's apartment house in Bremen (76, 195) yields to the inner needs for light and space toward the south, like the growth of a flower toward the sun. But generally speaking, for Wright the exterior and interior space of his invariably isolated buildings was continuous, and as he was an urbanophobe, the suburban environment of his buildings, when specifically regional, was not so particularly limiting spatially as an urban context. (The flowing plan of the Robie House, however, adapts to the constriction of the back sides of its corner lot.) Wright however, I believe, refused to recognize the setting that was not sympathetic to the direct expression of the interior. The Guggenheim Museum is an anomaly on Fifth Avenue. But the Johnson Wax Building perhaps makes a negative gesture toward its indifferent urban environment by dominating and excluding it.

Contrast and even conflict between exterior and interior forces exist outside architecture as well. Kepes has said: "Every phenomenon—a physical object, an organic form, a feeling, a thought, our group life—owes its shape and character to the duel between opposing tendencies; a physical configuration is a product of the duel between

82

195. Aalto. Apartment Building, Bremen

native constitution and outside environment."[43] This interplay has always been vivid in the concentrations of the urban environment. Wright's Morris Store (196, 197) is another one of the exceptions he was confident enough to make. Its strong contradictions between the inside and the outside—between the particular, private and the general, public functions, make it a traditional urban building rare in Modern architecture. As Aldo van Eyck says: "Planning on whatever scale level should provide a framework—to set the stage as it were—for the twin-phenomenon of the individual and the collective without resorting to arbitrary accentuation of either one at the expense of the other."[44]

Contradiction, or at least a contrast, between the inside and the outside is an essential characteristic of urban architecture, but it is not only an urban phenomenon. Besides the Villa Savoye and obvious examples like the domestic Greek temples of the Greek Revival which were crammed expediently with series of cells, the Renaissance villa such as Hawksmoor's Easton Neston or Westover in Virginia (198) juxtaposed symmetrical façades on asymmetrical plans.

Contradictory interplays between inside and outside spatial needs can be seen in the following examples in which the front and the back contrast. The diagram (199) illustrates six general cases. The concave façade in the Baroque church accommodates spatial needs that are specifically different on the inside and the outside. The concave exterior, at odds with the church's essential concave spatial function inside, acknowledges a contrasting exterior need for a spatial pause in the street. At the front of the building outside space is more important. Behind the façade the church was designed from the inside out, but in front it was designed from the outside in. The space left over by this contradiction was taken care of with poché. The plans of the two pavilions by Fischer von Erlach (200) illustrate through the concave curves in one the inside-dominant space and through the convex curves in the second the outside-dominant space. The concave façade of Lutyens' Grey Walls (56) accommodates an entrance court whose curve is determined by the turning radius of a car, and which concludes the vista of the approach. Grey Walls is a rural Piazza S. Ignazio (201). The concave exterior of Aalto's studio at Munkkiniemi (202) shapes an outdoor amphitheatre. These examples produce residual spaces inside.

Fischer von Erlach's Karlskirche (42), mentioned ear-

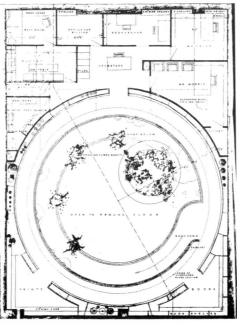

196. Wright. Morris Store, San Francisco. Plan

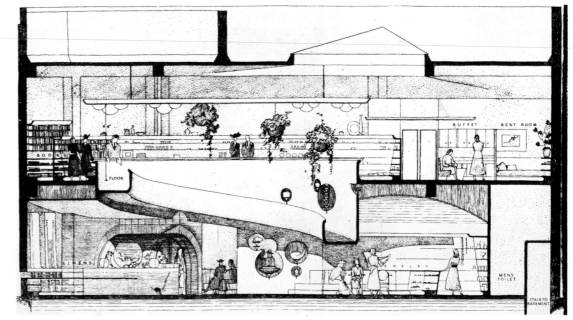

197. Wright. Morris Store, San Francisco. Section

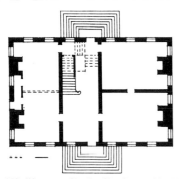

198. Westover, Charles City County, Va. Plan

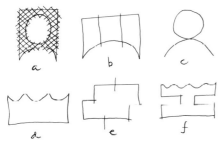

199. Façade diagrams

201. Raguzzini. Piazza S. Ignazio. Rome

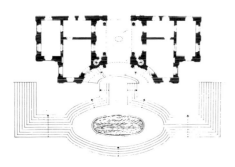

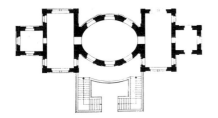

200. Fischer von Erlach. Two Pavilions. Plans

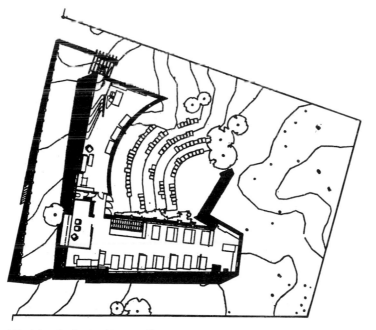

202. Aalto. Studio, Munkkiniemi. Plan

lier, combines a small oval church with a large rectangular façade that accommodates to its particular urban setting by means of a false façade rather than by poché. The concave façade of the garden pavilion of the Arcadian Academy in Rome (203) is in even more contradictory contrast to the villa behind it. The façade has been given its particular size and shape in order to terminate the terraced garden. In the Sanctuary of Saronno (204) there is contradiction in style as well as in scale between the façade and the rest of the building.

In the Baroque church the inside is different from the outside, but the back is also different from the front. American architecture, and especially Modern architecture with its antipathy to the "false front," has emphasized the freestanding, independent building even in the city—the building which is an isolated pavilion rather than one which reinforces the street line has become the norm. Johnson has called this the American tradition of "plop architecture." Aalto's dormitory at M.I.T. (205) is exceptional. The curving front along the river and its fenestration and materials contrast with the rectangularity and other characteristics of the rear: exterior as well as interior forces of use and space and structure vary back and front. And the P.S.F.S. building, which is a tower, has four different sides because it recognizes its specific urban setting: party walls, street façades—backs, fronts and corner. Here the freestanding building becomes a fragment of a greater exterior spatial whole, but the typical freestanding building of Modern architecture, except for some surface treatment and screens, which act to de-emphasize the spatial enclosure or to recognize orientation differences, seldom changes front and back for exterior spatial reasons. To the eighteenth century, also, this was a conventional idea. The ingenious double axis hotel in Paris (206), even in its originally more open setting, accommodated outside spaces differently at the front and back. With similar justification, Hawksmoor's Easton Neston (154) yields a tense disunity between front and side. The discontinuous elevation on the intimate garden side away from the long axis, accommodates varieties of spaces and levels inside and necessities of scale outside. The side elevation of the Strozzi Palace (207) anticipates its hidden position on a side alley.

Designing from the outside in, as well as the inside out, creates necessary tensions, which help make architecture. Since the inside is different from the outside, the wall

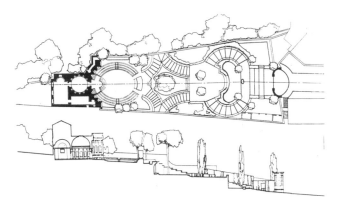

203. Arcadian Academy, Rome. Plan

204. Sanctuary of S. Maria dei Miracoli, Saronno

—the point of change—becomes an architectural event. Architecture occurs at the meeting of interior and exterior forces of use and space. These interior and environmental forces are both general and particular, generic and circumstantial. Architecture as the wall between the inside and the outside becomes the spatial record of this resolution and its drama. And by recognizing the difference between the inside and the outside, architecture opens the door once again to an urbanistic point of view.

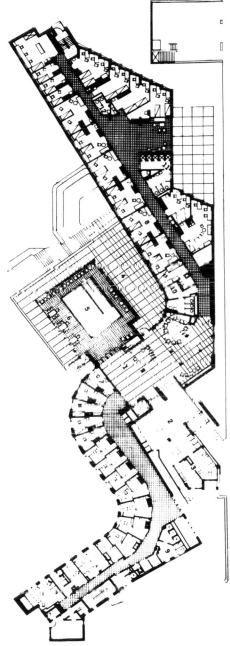

205. Aalto. Baker House Dormitory, M.I.T.,
Cambridge. Plan

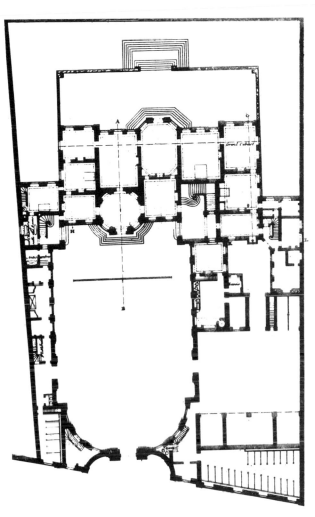

206. Courtonne. Hôtel de Matignon, Rue de Varenne, Paris. Plan

207. Maiano. Strozzi Palace, Florence. Perspective

. . . Toledo [Ohio] was very beautiful.*

An architecture of complexity and accommodation does not forsake the whole. In fact, I have referred to a special obligation toward the whole because the whole is difficult to achieve. And I have emphasized the goal of unity rather than of simplification in an art "whose . . . truth [is] in its totality."[45] It is the difficult unity through inclusion rather than the easy unity through exclusion. Gestalt psychology considers a perceptual whole the result of, and yet more than, the sum of its parts. The whole is dependent on the position, number, and inherent characteristics of the parts. A complex system in Herbert A. Simon's definition includes "a large number of parts that interact in a non-simple way."[46] The difficult whole in an architecture of complexity and contradiction includes multiplicity and diversity of elements in relationships that are inconsistent or among the weaker kinds perceptually.

Concerning the positions of the parts, for instance, such an architecture encourages complex and contrapuntal rhythms over simple and single ones. The "difficult whole" can include a diversity of directions as well. Concerning the number of parts in a whole, the two extremes—a single part and a multiplicity of parts—read as wholes most easily: the single part is itself a unity; and extreme multiplicity reads like a unity through a tendency of the parts to change scale, and to be perceived as an overall pattern or texture. The next easiest whole is the trinity: three is the commonest number of compositional parts making a monumental unity in architecture.

But an architecture of complexity and contradiction also embraces the "difficult" numbers of parts—the duality, and the medium degrees of multiplicity. If the program or structure dictates a combination of two elements within any of the varying scales of a building, this is an architecture which exploits the duality, and more or less resolves dualities into a whole. Our recent architecture has suppressed dualities. The loose composition of the whole used in the "binuclear plan" employed by some architects right after the Second World War, was only a partial exception to this rule. But our tendency to distort the program and to sub-

* Gertrude Stein, *Gertrude Stein's America*, Gilbert A. Harrison, ed., Robert B. Luce Inc., Washington, D. C., 1965.

vert the composition in order to disguise the duality is refuted by a tradition of accepted dualities, more or less resolved, at all scales of building and planning—from Gothic portals and Renaissance windows to the Mannerist façades of the sixteenth century and Wren's complex of pavilions at Greenwich Hospital. In painting, duality has had a continuous tradition—for example, in compositions of the Madonna and Child and of the Annunciation; in enigmatic Mannerist compositions such as Piero della Francesca's *Flagellation* (208); and in the recent work of Ellsworth Kelly (209), Morris Louis (210), and others.

Sullivan's Farmers' and Merchants' Union Bank in Columbus, Wisconsin (211), is exceptional in our recent architecture. The difficult duality is prominent. The plan reflects the bisected inside space which accommodates the public and the clerks on different sides of the counter running perpendicular to the façade. On the outside the door and the window at grade reflect this duality: they are themselves bisected by the shafts above. But the shafts, in turn, divide the lintel into a unity of three with a dominant central panel. The arch above the lintel tends to reinforce duality because it springs from the center of a panel below, yet by its oneness and its dominant size it also resolves the duality made by the window and the door. The façade is composed of the play of diverse numbers of parts—single elements as well as those divided into two or three are almost equally prominent—but the façade as a whole makes a unity.

Gestalt psychology also shows that the nature of the parts, as well as their number and position, influences a perceptual whole and it also has made a further distinction: the degree of wholeness can vary. Parts can be more or less whole in themselves, or, to put it in another way, in greater or lesser degree they can be fragments of a greater whole. Properties of the part can be more or less articulated; properties of the whole can be more or less accented. In the complex compositions, a special obligation toward the whole encourages the fragmentary part or, as Trystan Edwards calls it, the term, "inflection."[47]

Inflection in architecture is the way in which the whole is implied by exploiting the nature of the individual parts, rather than their position or number. By inflecting toward something outside themselves, the parts contain their own linkage: inflected parts are more integral with the whole than are *un*inflected parts. Inflection is a means

208. Piero della Francesca. *Flagellation of Christ*. ca. 1455–60

209. Kelly. *Green, Blue, Red*. 1964

210. Louis. *Theta*. 1960

211. Sullivan. Farmers' and Merchants' Union Bank, Columbus, Wis.

of distinguishing diverse parts while implying continuity. It involves the art of the fragment. The valid fragment is economical because it implies richness and meaning beyond itself. Inflection can also be used to achieve suspense, an element possible in large sequential complexes. The inflected element can be called a partial-functioning element in contrast to the double-functioning element. In terms of perception it is dependent on something outside itself, and in whose direction it inflects. It is a directional form corresponding to directional space.

The interior of the church of the Madonna del Calcinaio in Cortona (137) is composed of a limited number of elements which are uninflected. Its windows and niches (212), pilasters and pediments, and the articulated elements of its altar, are independent wholes, simple in themselves and symmetrical in form and position. They add up to a greater whole. The interior of the pilgrimage church at Birnau in Bavaria (213), however, contains a diversity of inflections directed toward the altar. The complex curves of the vaults and arches, even the distortions of the pilaster capitals, inflect toward this center. The statues and the multitude of fragmental elements of the side altars (214) are inflected parts, asymmetrical in form yet symmetrical in position, which integrate into a symmetrical whole. This subordination of parts corresponds to Wölfflin's "unified unity" of the Baroque—which he contrasts with the "multiple unity" of the Renaissance.

A comparison of the entrance fronts of Blenheim Palace (215) and Holkham Hall (216) illustrates the use of inflection on the exterior. Holkham Hall achieves an extensive whole through the addition of similar wholes which are always independent: most of its bays are pedimented pavilions which could stand alone as single buildings—Holkham Hall could almost be three buildings in a row. Blenheim achieves a complex whole through fragmental parts, separate but inflected. The last two bays of the central block, when taken alone, are dualities incomplete in themselves. But in relation to the whole they become inflected terminations to the central pavilion, and a confirmation of the pedimented center of the whole composition. The piers at the corners of the porch and the broken pediments above them are also terminal inflections, similarly reinforcing the center. The bays at the far extremities of this enormous façade form pavilions which are not inflected. They are perhaps expressive of the relative inde-

212. Martini. Church of the Madonna del Calcinaio, Cortona

213. Thumb. Church, Birnau, Lake Constance, Bavaria

214. Thumb. Church, Birnau, Lake Constance, Bavaria

215. Vanbrugh. Blenheim Palace, Oxfordshire. Elevation

216. Kent. Holkham Hall, Norfolk. Elevation

pendence of the kitchen and stable wings. Vanbrugh's method of creating a strong whole in such a large and diverse if symmetrical façade follows the traditional Jacobean method of the century before: at Aston Hall (217) the wings of the forecourt façade and the towers, parapeted pediments, and windows inflect in position and/or shape toward its center.

The varying configurations of the wings and windows, roofs and ornaments of the orphanage of the Buon Pastore near Rome (218, 219, 220) are an orgy of inflections of enormous scope similar to the scale of Blenheim. This neo-Baroque complex by Armando Brazini, (bizarre in 1940 and admittedly questionable for an asylum for little girls) astonishingly composes a multitude of diverse parts into a difficult whole. At all levels of scale it is an example of inflections within inflections successively directed toward different centers—toward the short façade in the front, or the anticlimactically small dome near the center of the complex, with its unusually big cupola. When you stand close enough to see a smaller element of inflection, you sometimes need to turn almost 180 degrees to see its counterpart at a great distance. An element of suspense is introduced when you move around the enormous building. You are aware of elements related by inflection to elements already seen or not yet seen, like the unraveling of a symphony. As a fragment in plan and elevation, the asymmetrical composition of each wing is wrought with tensions and implications concerning the symmetrical whole.

At the scale of the town, inflection can come from the position of elements which are in themselves uninflected. In the Piazza del Popolo (221) the domes of the twin churches confirm each building as a separate whole, but their single towers, symmetrical themselves, become inflective because of their asymmetrical positions on each church. In the context of the piazza each building is a fragment of a greater whole and a part of a gateway to the Corso. At the smaller scale of Palladio's Villa Zeno (222) the asymmetrical positions of the symmetrical arched openings cause the end pavilions to inflect toward the center, thus enforcing the symmetry of the whole composition. This kind of inflection of asymmetrical ornament within a symmetrical whole is a dominant motif in Rococo architecture. For example, on the side altars at Birnau (214), and on the characteristic pairs of sconces (223), or andirons, doors, or other elements, the inflection of the rocaille is part of an

217. Hatfield and Blickling. Aston Hall, Birmingham

218. Brazini. Orphanage of Il Buon Pastore, near Rome

219. Brazini. Orphanage of Il Buon Pastore, near Rome

220. Brazini. Orphanage of Il Buon Pastore, near Rome

221. Piazza del Popolo, Rome. Sketch

222. Palladio. Villa Zeno, Cessalto. Elevation

223. Rococo Sconce

asymmetry within a larger symmetry that exaggerates the unity yet creates a tension in the whole.

Direction is a means of inflection in the Villa Aldobrandini (224). Its front is articulated into additive parts or bays, but the unique diagonals of the fragmentary pediments on the end bays tend to direct the ends toward the center, and unify that dominating façade. In the plan of Monticello (225) the enclosing diagonal walls inflect the extremities toward the center focus. In Siena the distortion of its façade inflects the Palazzo Pubblico (226) toward its dominating piazza. Here distortion is a method of confirming the whole rather than of breaking it, as in the case of contradiction accommodated. Baroque details, such as coupled pilasters in the end bays of a series of pilastered bays, become devices of inflection because they create variations in rhythm to terminate a sequence. Such methods of inflection are largely used to confirm the whole—and since monumentality involves a strong expression of the whole, as well as a certain kind of scale, inflection becomes a device of monumentality as well.

Inflection accommodates the difficult whole of a duality as well as the easier complex whole. It is a way of resolving a duality. The inflecting towers on the twin churches on the Piazza del Popolo resolve the duality by implying that the center of the whole composition is located in the space of the bisecting Corso. In Wren's Royal Hospital at Greenwich (227) the inflection of the domes by their asymmetrical position similarly resolves the duality of the enormous masses flanking the Queen's House. Their inflection further enhances the centrality and importance of this diminutive building. The unresolved dualities of the end pavilions facing the river, on the other hand, reinforce the unifying quality of the central axis by their own contrasting disunity.

The French chevet contrasts with the blunt termination of the English Gothic choir, because it inflects to terminate and enhance the whole. In the church of the Jacobins in Toulouse (228) the inflection of the chevet tends to resolve the duality of the nave, which is bisected by the row of columns. The apse in Furness' library at the University of Pennsylvania similarly resolves the duality formed by the arched interior wall opposite. One column bisects the nave at the end of the Late Gothic parish church at Dingolfing (229), a hall-type church, but the juxtaposition of the central bay and window behind, which evolve

224. Della Porta and Domenichino. Villa Aldobrandini, Frascati. Perspective

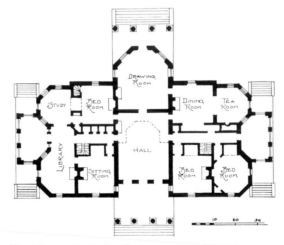
225. Jefferson. Monticello, Charlottesville. Plan

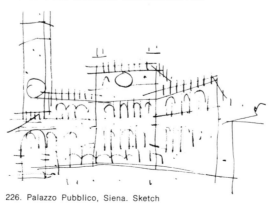
226. Palazzo Pubblico, Siena. Sketch

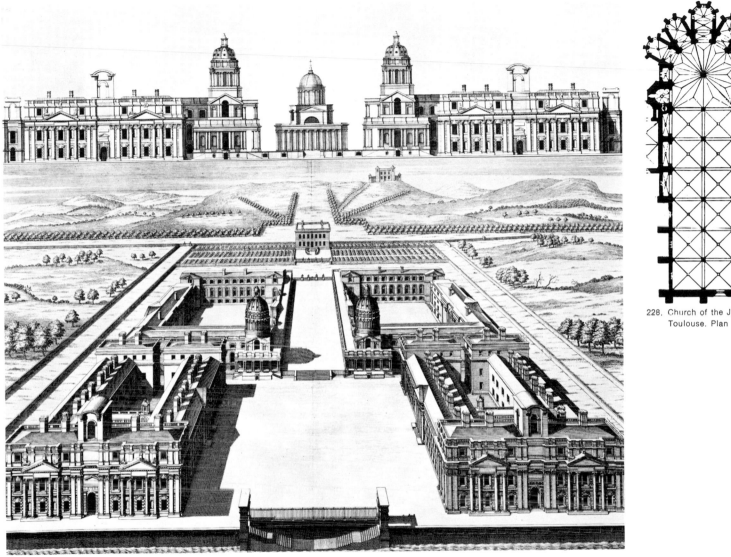

227. Wren and Jones. Royal Hospital, Greenwich. Perspective

228. Church of the Jacobins,
Toulouse. Plan

from the complex vaulting above, resolve the original duality. The directional inflecting of the side walls of the nave of the parish church in Rimella (230) counteracts the disunifying effect of the two bays of the nave. Their inflection toward the center increases enclosure and strengthens the whole. A minor intermediate bay also binds the major bays together.

Lutyens' work abounds in dualities. The duality of the entrance façade of the castle at Lambay (231), for instance, is resolved by the inflecting shape of the opening in the juxtaposed garden wall. In contemporary architecture rare examples of inflection are found in the vestigial broken pediments of Moretti's apartment house on the Via Parioli (10). They partially resolve the duality of the pair of wings which distinguish sets of apartments. The subtly balanced duality of Wright's Unity Temple (232) is devoid of inflections unless the directional entrance pedestal is one.

Modern architecture tends to reject inflection at all levels of scale. In the Tugendhat House no inflecting capital compromises the purity of the column's form, although the shear forces in the supported roof plane must thus be ignored. Walls are inflected neither by bases nor cornices nor by structural reinforcements, such as quoins, at corners. Mies' pavilions are as independent as Greek temples; Wright's wings are interdependent but interlocked rather than independent and inflected. However, Wright, in accommodating his rural buildings to their particular sites, has recognized inflection at the scale of the whole building. For example, Fallingwater is incomplete without its context—it is a fragment of its natural setting which forms the greater whole. Away from its setting it would have no meaning.

If inflection can occur at many scales—from a detail of a building to a whole building—it can contain varying degrees of intensity as well. Moderate degrees of inflection have a kind of implied continuity that affirms the whole. Extreme inflection literally becomes continuity. Today we emphasize our opportunities to express the literal continuities of structure and materials—such as the welded joint, skin structures, and reinforced concrete. Except for the flush joint of early Modern architecture, implied continuity is rare. The shadow joint of Mies' vocabulary tends to exaggerate separation. And Wright, especially, articulates a joint by a change in profile when there is a change in

229. Parish Church, Dingolfing, W. Germany

230. Parish Church, Rimella. Plan

231. Lutyens. Lambay Castle, Ireland

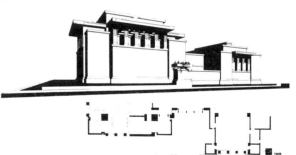

232. Wright. Unity Temple, Oak Park. Plan and elevation

material—an expressive manifestation of the nature of materials in Organic architecture. But a contrast between expressive continuity and real discontinuity of structure and materials is a characteristic of the façade of Saarinen's dormitory at the University of Pennsylvania. In section its continuous curves defy the changes in materials, structure, and use. In the precise walls of Machu Picchu (233) the same profile continues between the built-up jointed masonry and the rock in situ. The arched shape of the opening of Ledoux's entrance at Bourneville (58) spans two kinds of structure (corbeled and arched) and two kinds of material (rusticated masonry at the top and smooth masonry at the bottom). Similar contradictions occur in Rococo furniture. Cabriole legs (234) disguise the joint and express continuity in their shape and ornament. The continuous grooves common to the leg and the seat-frame imply a continuity beyond inflection which is somewhat contradictory to the material and the structural relationship of these separate frame elements. The ubiquitous rocaille is another ornamental device for expressive continuity common to the architecture and furniture of the Rococo.

Some of Wright's early interiors (235) parallel in the motif of the wood strip the rocaille-filled interiors of the Rococo (236). In Unity Temple and the Evans House (235) these strips are used on the furniture, walls, ceilings, light fixtures, and window mullions, and the pattern is repeated on the rugs. As in the Rococo, a continuous motif is used to achieve a strong whole expressive of what Wright called plasticity. He employed a method of implied continuity for valid expressive reasons, and in ironic contradiction to his dogma of the nature of materials and his expressed hatred of the Rococo.

On the other hand, an architecture of complexity and contradiction can acknowledge an expressive *dis*continuity, which belies a certain structural continuity. In the choir screen in the cathedral at Modena (237), where one uninflected element precariously supports another in its visual expression, or in the abrupt abutments of the uninflected wings of All Saints Church, Margaret Street (93), a formal discontinuity is implied where there is a structural continuity. Soane's Gate at Langley Park (238) is made up of three architectural elements totally uninflected and independent; besides the dominance of the middle element, it is the sculptural elements which are inflected and which give unity to the three parts.

233. Walls, Machu Picchu, Peru

235. Wright. Evans House, Chicago

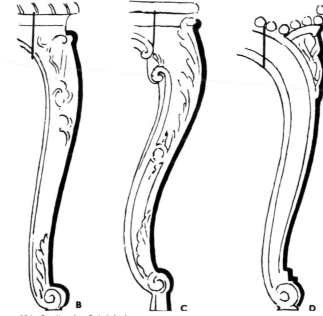

234. Studies for Cabriole Legs

236. Cuvilliés. Amalienburg Pavilion, Nymphenburg Palace, near Munich

238. Soane. Gateway, Langley Park, Norfolk

237. Modena Cathedral

The Doric order (239) works a complex balance among extremes of both expressive and structural continuities and discontinuities. The architrave, the capital, and the shaft are noncontinuous structurally but only partially noncontinuous expressively. That the architrave sits on the capital is expressed by the uninflected abacus. But the echinus in relation to the shaft expresses structural continuity consistent with expressive continuity. The horizontal and vertical elements of Saarinen's T.W.A. Terminal and Frederick Kiesler's Endless House are without structural contradiction: they are continuous everywhere. However, precast concrete that is assembled offers ambiguous combinations of continuity and discontinuity, both structural and expressive. The surfaces of the Police Administration Building in Philadelphia include patterns of shadow joints separating precast elements whose curving inflections, however, evolve continuous profiles—a paradoxical play of continuity and discontinuity inherent in the expression and the structure of the architecture.

A kind of implied continuity or inflection is inherent in Maki's "group form." This, the third category in the designation of complex architecture he calls "collective form," includes "generative" parts with their own "linkage," and wholes in which the system and unit are integral. He has referred to other characteristics of group form which indicate some of the implications of inflection in architecture. A consistency of the basic parts and their sequential relationship permit a growth in time, a consistency of human scale, and a sensitivity to the particular topography of the complex.

The "group form" contrasts with Maki's other basic category, the "mega-form." The whole, which is dominated by hierarchical relationships of parts rather than by the inherent inflective nature of the parts, can also be a characteristic of complex architecture. Hierarchy is implicit in an architecture of many levels of meaning. It involves configurations of configurations—the interrelationships of several orders of varying strengths to achieve a complex whole. In the plan of Christ Church, Spitalfields (240), it is the sequence of orders of supports—higher, lower, and middle; large, small, and medium—that make the hierarchical whole. Or in a palace façade of Palladio (48), it is the juxtapositions and adjacencies of parts (pilasters, windows, and mouldings) and the contrasts of large, small, and relatively important that conduct the eye to the whole.

The dominant binder is another manifestation of the hierarchical relationships of parts. It manifests itself in the consistent pattern (the thematic kind of order) as well as by being the dominant element. This is not a difficult whole to achieve. In the context of an architecture of contradiction it can be a doubtful panacea, like the fallen snow which unifies a chaotic landscape. At a scale of the town in the Medieval period it is the wall or castle which is the dominant element. In the Baroque it is the axis of the street against which minor diversities play. (In Paris the rigid axis is confirmed by cornice heights, while in Rome the axis tends to zigzag and is punctuated by connecting piazzas with obelisks.) The axial binder in Baroque planning sometimes reflects a program devised by an autocracy, which could easily exclude elements that today must be considered. Arterial circulation can be a dominant device in contemporary urban planning. In fact, in the program the consistent binder is most often represented by circulation, and in construction the consistent binder is usually the major order of structure. It is an important device of Kahn's viaduct architecture and Tange's collective forms for Tokyo. The dominant binder is an expediency in renovations. James Ackerman has referred to Michelangelo's predilection for "symmetrical juxtaposition of diagonal accents in plan and elevation" in his design for St. Peter's, which was essentially a renovation of earlier construction. "By using diagonal wall-masses to fuse together the arms of the cross, Michelangelo was able to give St. Peter's a unity that earlier designs lacked." [48]

The dominant binder, as a third element connecting a duality, is a less difficult way of resolving a duality than inflection. For example, the big arch unambiguously resolves the duality of the double window of the Florentine Renaissance palazzo. The façade of the double church of S. Antonio and S. Brigidá by Fuga (241) is resolved by inflected broken pediments—but also by a third ornamental element, which dominates the middle. Similarly, the façade of S. Maria della Spina, Pisa (242) is dominated by a third pediment. In plan the domed bays of Guarini's church of the Immaculate Conception in Turin (14) are inflected in shape, but they are also resolved by a minor intermediate bay. The ornamental pediment at the center of the elevation of Charleval (243) is also a dominant third element, as are the gable and the stair at the front of the farmer's house near Chieti (244)—similar, in this context, to the

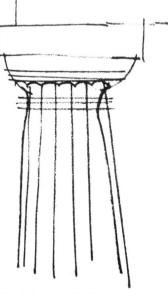

239. Doric order. Sketch

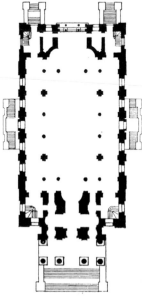

240. Hawksmoor. Christ Church, Spitalfields. Plan

241. Fuga. Church of S. Antonio and S. Brígida. Elevation study

242. S. Maria della Spina, Pisa

245. Stratford Hall, Westmoreland County, Va.

243. Du Cerceau. Château, Charleval. Elevation

244. Farmer's House, near Chieti

246. Vignola. Villa Lante, Bagnaia. Plan

function of the stair to the entrance of Stratford Hall, Virginia (245). There is no inflection in the composition of the Villa Lante (246), but an axis between the two equal pavilions, which focuses on a sculpture placed at a cross-axis, dominates the twin pavilions as a third element, thus emphasizing a whole.

But a more ambiguously hierarchical relationship of uninflected parts creates a more difficult perceptual whole. Such a whole is composed of equal combinations of parts. While the idea of equal combinations is related to the phenomenon both-and, and many examples apply to both ideas, both-and refers more specifically to contradiction in architecture, while equal combinations refer more to unity. With equal combinations the whole does not depend on inflection, or the easier relationships of the dominant binder, or motival consistency. For example, in the Porta Pia (110, 111) the number of each kind of element in the composition of the door and the wall is almost equal—no one element dominates. The varieties of shapes (rectangular, square, triangular, segmental, and round) being almost equal, the predominance of any one shape is also precluded, and the equal varieties of directions (vertical, horizontal, diagonal, and curving) have the same effect. There is similarly an equal diversity in the size of the elements. The equal combinations of parts achieve a whole through superimposition and symmetry rather than through dominance and hierarchy.

The window above Sullivan's portal in the Merchants' National Bank in Grinnell, Iowa (112), is almost identical to the Porta Pia in its juxtaposition of an equal number of round, square and diamond-shaped frames of equal size. The diverse combinations of number analyzed in his Columbia Bank façade (groups of elements involving one, two, and three parts) have almost equal value in the composition. However, there the unity is based upon the relation of horizontal layers rather than on superimposition. The Auditorium (104) exploits the complexity of directions and rhythms that such a program can yield. The simple semicircles of the wall ornament, structure, and segmental ceiling coves counteract, in plan and section, the complex curves of the proscenium arches, rows of seats, balcony slopes, boxes, and column brackets. These, in turn, play against the rectangular relationships of ceilings, walls, and columns.

This sense of the equivocal in much of Sullivan's work (at least where the program is more complex than that of a skyscraper) points up another contrast between him and Wright. Wright would seldom express the contradiction inherent in equal combinations. Instead, he resolved all sizes and shapes into a motival order—a single predominant order of circles or rectangles or diagonals. The Vigo Schmidt House project is a consistent pattern of triangles, the Ralph Jester House of circles, and the Paul Hanna House of hexagons.

Equal combinations are used to achieve a whole in Aalto's complex Cultural Center at Wolfsburg (78). He does not disperse the parts nor make them similar as Mies does at I.I.T. As I have pointed out before, he achieves a whole by combining an almost equal number of diagonal and rectangular elements. S. Maria delle Grazie in Milan (247) works equal combinations into an extreme form by contrasting opposite shapes in its exterior composition. The dominant triangle-rectangle composition in the front combines with the dominant circle-square composition in the back. Michelucci's church of the Autostrada (4), like the Church of the Holy Sepulchre in Jerusalem (plan only

illustrated in 101), consists of almost equal combinations of contrasting directions and rhythms in columns, piers, walls, and roofs. A similar composition is that of the Berlin Philharmonic Hall (248). The plastic forms of indigenous Mediterranean architecture (249) are simple in texture, but rectangles, diagonals, and segments are blatantly combined. Gaudí's dressing table in the Casa Güell (250) represents an orgy of contrasting dualities of form: extreme inflection and continuity are combined with violent adjacencies and discontinuities, complex and simple curves, rectangles and diagonals, contrasting materials, symmetry and asymmetry, in order to accommodate a multiplicity of functions in one whole. At the scale of furniture, the prevalent sense of the equivocal is expressed in the chair illustrated in (103). Its back configuration is curving and its front is rectangular. It is not dissimilar in its difficult composition to Aalto's bentwood chair illustrated in (251).

Inherent in an architecture of opposites is the inclusive whole. The unity of the interior of the Imatra church or the complex at Wolfsburg is achieved not through suppression or exclusion but through the dramatic inclusion of contradictory or circumstantial parts. Aalto's architecture acknowledges the difficult and subtle conditions of program, while "serene" architecture, on the other hand, works simplifications.

However, the obligation toward the whole in an architecture of complexity and contradiction does not preclude the building which is unresolved. Poets and playwrights acknowledge dilemmas without solutions. The validity of the questions and vividness of the meaning are what make their works art more than philosophy. A goal of poetry can be unity of expression over resolution of content. Contemporary sculpture is often fragmentary, and today we appreciate Michelangelo's unfinished Pietàs more than his early work, because their content is suggested, their expression more immediate, and their forms are completed beyond themselves. A building can also be more or less incomplete in the expression of its program and its form.

The Gothic cathedral, like Beauvais, for instance, of which only the enormous choir was built, is frequently unfinished in relation to its program, yet it is complete in the effect of its form because of the motival consistency of its many parts. The complex program which is a process, continually changing and growing in time yet at each stage at some level related to a whole, should be recognized as

247. Bramante and Solari. S. Maria delle Grazie, Milan

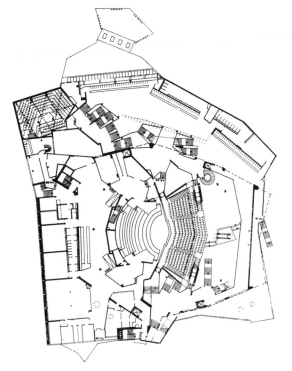

248. Scharoun. Philharmonic Hall, Berlin. Plan

249. Houses, Naples

250. Gaudí. Dressing Table, Casa Güell, Barcelona

essential at the scale of city planning. The incomplete program is valid for a complex single building as well.

Each of the fragmental twin churches on the Piazza del Popolo, however, is complete at the level of program but incomplete in the expression of form. The uniquely asymmetrically placed tower, as we have seen, inflects each building toward a greater whole outside itself. The very complex building, which in its open form is incomplete, in itself relates to Maki's "group form;" it is the antithesis of the "perfect single building" [49] or the closed pavilion. As a fragment of a greater whole in a greater context this kind of building relates again to the scope of city planning as a means of increasing the unity of the complex whole. An architecture that can simultaneously recognize contradictory levels should be able to admit the paradox of the whole fragment: the building which is a whole at one level and a fragment of a greater whole at another level.

251. Aalto. Bentwood and Metal Chair. 1929–33

252. Jefferson. University of Virginia, Charlottesville

In *God's Own Junkyard* Peter Blake has compared the chaos of commercial Main Street with the orderliness of the University of Virginia (252, 253). Besides the irrelevancy of the comparison, is not Main Street almost all right? Indeed, is not the commercial strip of a Route 66 almost all right? As I have said, our question is: what slight twist of context will make them all right? Perhaps more signs more contained. Illustrations in *God's Own Junkyard* of Times Square and roadtown are compared with illustrations of New England villages and arcadian countrysides. But the pictures in this book that are supposed to be bad are often good. The seemingly chaotic juxtapositions of honky-tonk elements express an intriguing kind of vitality and validity, and they produce an unexpected approach to unity as well.

It is true that an ironic interpretation such as this results partly from the change in scale of the subject matter in photographic form and the change in context within the frames of the photographs. But in some of these compositions there is an inherent sense of unity not far from the surface. It is not the obvious or easy unity derived from the dominant binder or the motival order of simpler, less contradictory compositions, but that derived from a complex and illusive order of the difficult whole. It is the taut composition which contains contrapuntal relationships, equal combinations, inflected fragments, and acknowledged dualities. It is the unity which "maintains, but only just maintains, a control over the clashing elements which compose it. Chaos is very near; its nearness, but its avoidance, gives . . . force." [50] In the validly complex building or cityscape, the eye does not want to be too easily or too quickly satisfied in its search for unity within a whole.

Some of the vivid lessons of Pop Art, involving contradictions of scale and context, should have awakened architects from prim dreams of pure order, which, unfortunately, are imposed in the easy Gestalt unities of the urban renewal projects of establishment Modern architecture and yet, fortunately are really impossible to achieve at any great scope. And it is perhaps from the everyday landscape, vulgar and disdained, that we. can draw the complex and contradictory order that is valid and vital for our architecture as an urbanistic whole.

253. Typical Main Street, U.S.A.

1. Project, Pearson House, Chestnut Hill, Pa., Robert Venturi, 1957. (254–259)

This project for a house was designed in 1957. It is a rare manifestation of the idea of multiple enclosure in my work because layers of enclosure require programs of a scale which I have not yet had the opportunity to exploit. It involves things in things and things behind things. It exploits the idea of contrasting spatial layers between the inside and the outside in the series of parallel walls in plan and in the open inner domes supported on diagonal frames in section; the idea of contrapuntal, rhythmic juxtaposition in the relation of the pier openings of the porch, and of the lower and upper windows and of the cupolas above the inner domes; and the idea of a series of spaces en suite which are general in shape and unspecific in function, separated by servant spaces specific in shape and function.

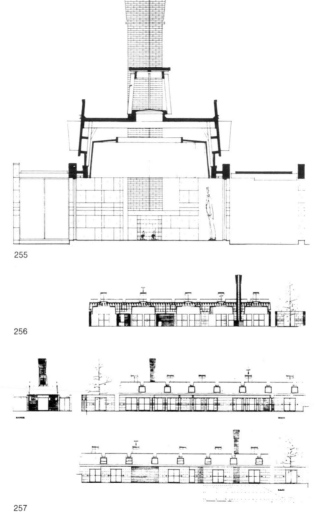

255

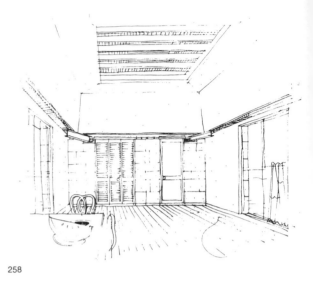

258

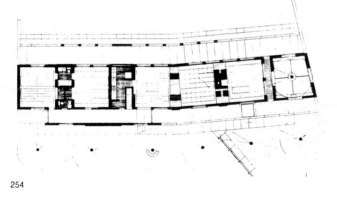

254

256

257

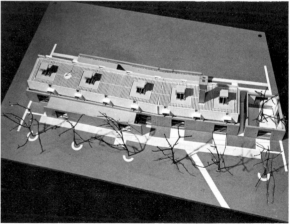

259

2. Renovations of the James B. Duke House, The Institute of Fine Arts, New York University, Robert Venturi, Cope and Lippincott, Associated Architects, 1959. (260–264)

This mansion on upper Fifth Avenue was donated to the Institute of Fine Arts for use as a graduate school of the History of Art. It was designed by Horace Trumbauer in 1912; its interiors are by Alavoine. It is a copy of the Hôtel Labottière in Bordeaux on the outside, but it is blown up in scale and expanded in size—a Louis XIV scale in a Louis XVI building. Its Edwardian–Louis XVI details are exceptionally fine inside and out.

Our approach was to touch the inside as little as possible and to create harmony between the old and the new through contrasting juxtapositions: to separate the joint between the old and the new layers, to create change by adding to rather than modifying existing interior elements, to consider the new elements furniture rather than architecture and to use furniture and equipment which is commonplace and standard but enhanced by its uncommon setting. These elements are the bentwood chairs, and steel library shelving by Remington Rand whose rectangular geometry was superimposed on that of the wall panels, but separated from them by specially designed brass brackets with a sliding detail to avoid the mouldings and—from the floor—by specially designed feet for the posts.

260

261

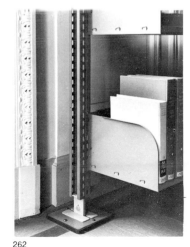

262

263

264

3. A Project for a Beach House, Robert Venturi, 1959. (265–271)

This weekend cottage, set among dunes on a beach, is to face the view of the ocean. It contains the simplest living accommodations, since the inhabitants are expected to spend most of the day on the beach. There is a small terrace on the ocean front and an open belvedere on the roof accessible by ladder and trap near the chimney.

The walls are balloon frame. The roof is wood-plank, toenailed so that the whole structure is a skin and a quasi-frame at the same time. An exception occurs at the inverse clerestory and at the front opening, where the span is exceptionally long, and where there are some expedient frame members: one post and some beams. This exception at the center makes the overall skin structure more apparent. (The floor is raised on wood piles and beams.)

Expressively, the house has only two elevations: the front, oriented toward the sea, and the back for entering. It has no sides, so to speak; and the front is different from the back to express its directional inflection toward the ocean view. The fireplace-chimney at the rear center is a focus for the diagonal walls, which radiate, at first symmetrically, to form the inner spaces. Because of these complex configurations in elevation and plan, the roof is hipped and gabled at the same time, and its original symmetrical form is distorted at the extremities of the building by varying interior demands, and by exterior forces of orientation and view. At the pointed end, the exterior spatial-expressive demands of a house "without sides," directed toward the view, dominate the secondary spatial needs of a shower inside.

The whole outside surface is natural cedar shingles. Barge boards at the juncture of the roof and wall are minimized to make roof and wall look more continuous. The overlapping scales of the walls end in a skirt over the piles. Windows and porch openings punch varying holes in the continuous skin. The interior surfaces, which you see beyond the windows and within the porch, are contrastingly painted board surfaces, like the inside lining of a cape. The soffits of the openings, where the skin is cut, are painted a contrasting color. The shingles never touch the block chimney and its buttress, which divides near its base, and forms an open vestibule as well.

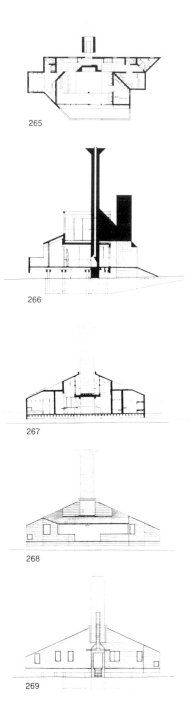

265

266

267

268

269

270

271

4. Headquarters Building, North Penn Visiting Nurse Association, Venturi and Short, 1960. (272–277)

Economy dictated a small building with conventional construction. The setting suggested a bold scale and a simple form to compensate for the large buildings around. The program dictated a complex inside, however, with varieties of spaces and special storage accommodations. Level parking for five staff cars on the steeply sloping site necessitated a retaining-walled auto court up front. And a pedestrian entrance with a minimum of outside steps similarly dictated a building immediately on the street.

The resultant building is a distorted box both simple and complex. Because they are adjacent and similar in area, the court and the building set up a duality. The prow of the building acts as an inflection toward the court to resolve the duality, yet this distortion of the boxlike building simultaneously enforces the duality by complementing the curved wall at the opposite side of the parking court and by making the court more symmetrical and, therefore, independent of the building. The building at this point is more sculptural than architectural. Outside spatial forces dominate the interior forces, and it is designed from the outside in. The "awkward" interior created here is a subordinate space—merely the dentist's dark room.

Distortion works in the open side of the duality too: the slight curve of the retaining wall of the essentially rectangular court acknowledges and resists the pressure of the earth behind. The building box is distorted further by the east wall being parallel to the property line on this half-urban site. The surface of this originally plain box is also distorted. The windows on the front eat into it to provide integral overhangs toward the south. They also work integrally with the interior storage cabinets along that wall parallel to the roof framing.

The window indentations become large and few, sometimes coupled as well as set back, and they increase the scale of the small building. On the outside the scale of the lower windows is increased by the device of an extended frame—in this case, an applied wood moulding which accommodates the contradiction between the inside and outside scales. The complex positioning of the windows and openings of this façade also counteracts the simplicity of the box. They are not random but rather an originally regular rhythmic series distorted by interior complexities

and circumstances.

The entrance on the court side at an intermediate landing is similarly complex in composition and bold in scale. It is made up almost equally of rectangular, diagonal, and segmental elements juxtaposed in a manner similar to some Renaissance doors. The rectangularity of the overall opening results from the block and plank structure of the building. In contrast the arch derives not from the nature of the materials and structure of its wood frame but from its symbolism as an entrance. Furthermore, and more important, as a circumstantial exception to the general order of the composition, it becomes a focus. The diagonal posts are expediencies similarly eventful: they shore up the center beam which supports the exceptional span of the roof planks at this opening, and they contrast with the post, which is vertical in the large window opening in the front, and more analogous in its position to the rectangular composition of the building. The big opening of the arch, appropriate in scale for a civic building, is juxtaposed upon the man-scaled doors, which are sheltered. There is a juxtaposition here of scales as well as shapes.

As for the program complexities of the interior, a hint of the storage intricacies is confirmed in the alternating recessions of windows and closets in the front. Another manifestation is the diagonal wall in the plan of the hall—another expedient distortion to accommodate the program complexities, which are squeezed inside their rigid enclosure.

The inconsistent floor and roof structure is similarly accommodating to the bearing walls of the rigid perimeter. The first floor front is a two-way slab accommodating the irregular interior bearing walls. Steel and wood joists for the floors and roof otherwise run variously parallel with the walls containing window storage combinations. Here, as in the entrance opening, the span is wood planks, which permit openings and windows to reach the thin cornice line and make the box look more abstract. I have already mentioned the expedient post, vertical or diagonal, used when these surface spans become exceptionally long.

To emphasize thinness of surface and contradict the plasticity of the form of the box, the stucco surface is detailed with a minimum of corner-turnings by means of the wood-surfaced window reveals. I have "destroyed the box," not through spatial continuities but by circumstantial distortions.

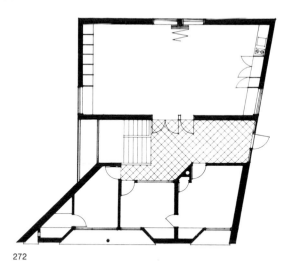

272

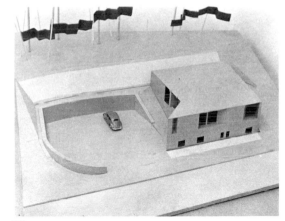

273

274

276

275

277

5. F.D.R. Memorial Competition, Robert Venturi, John Rauch, George Patton, and Nicholas Gianopulos, 1960. (278–283)

This is a directional earth form that contrasts and thereby enhances the white sculptural forms of the three major Washington memorials already existing in the neighborhood. It is not a fourth sculptural form next to a parking lot. It is several things at once: an open, white marble promenade along the Potomac, which recognizes and utilizes the river's edge for pedestrians; an integral street, which accommodates the visitors' parking and is enclosed by canyon-like walls contrasting with the open avenues around; and, on the other side, it is a green grass mound which is a background for the cherry trees on the basin. The complex curve of the vertical section on the riverside accommodates a multiplicity of ramps, stairs, and passages, and a surface in bas-relief, which is interesting close-up—yet by its extreme continuity, suggested and actual, this curve contributes a scale appropriately monumental and visible from a distance. On the other side the continuous curve in section accommodates varying materials—grass, ground cover, vine, and concrete cap, in sequence and in relation to the varying degrees of the slope. A variety of spaces is afforded by the sequence of open park: tight vehicular canyon, close pedestrian passage, and open directional promenade, in turn relieved by details like trees and benches, and at the middle, on axis with the Washington obelisk, by a vision slit spanned by a little vehicular bridge.

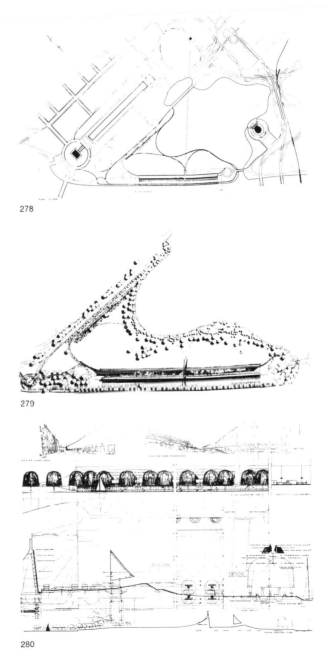

278

279

280

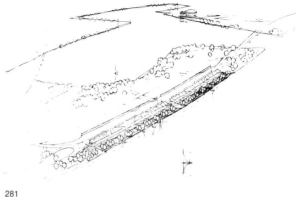

281

282

280

6. Renovation of Restaurant in West Philadelphia, Venturi and Short, 1962. (284–288)

The design of this restaurant involved the renovation of two adjacent dilapidated row houses whose first floor fronts had been previously converted into shops. The restaurant was to be a modest neighborhood place that catered to students. The owners stipulated that it was to retain the simple atmosphere of the former establishment a block away, which had been known as "Mom's," where students "would feel comfortable in their T-shirts." The budget was to (and finally did) match the modest character of the place.

In the interior as well as on the façade, we acknowledged rather than disguised the duality of the existing layout with its bearing party-wall down the middle. Another design determinant was a second, parallel bearing-wall, which came to divide the small serving area from the kitchen. The west side accommodates the dining room with booths and tables; the east side the kitchen, serving areas, toilets, counter, and entry. Beyond the vestibule at the entry there are interior steps, which make the transition to the higher level of the first floor of the former houses. On the extreme east side is the foyer to the future apartments above.

We decided to exploit rather than disguise the modest budget, and in keeping with the modest character of the place in which catsup bottles dot every table, we tended to use conventional means and elements throughout but in such a way as to make the common things take on a new meaning in their new context. This was also a reaction to the typically over-designed "modern" fixtures available today. For the main lighting fixtures we used large-size white porcelain R.L.M.'s—an old-fashioned industrial fixture that is solid but cheap and, in the context we gave it, elegant. The chairs were Thonet bentwood, which are also almost anonymously designed objects, although now perhaps becoming chi-chi. The booths were designed not as the exaggeratedly low, pseudo-luxuriously upholstered types that expose the sitter but as the more traditional, high kind with comfortable but modest padding and with an appropriate sense of privacy. The air conditioning ducts were exposed for economy and to create the same kind of incidental functional ornament that developed from the exposed mechanical ceiling fans of the past. The ceiling is acoustic tile,

the floors tinted concrete and resilient tile.

The wall ornamentation consists of surprisingly cheap painted patterns on the plaster above the wainscoting of the booths. The patterns of the letters spelling the proprietor's name, which extend almost the whole length of the room, have the character of conventional stencils. On the facing wall a direct reflection is juxtaposed against the "windows" to the open kitchen. These illogicalities emphasize the more ornamental function of the typography. The enormous letters create a scale and unity appropriate to a public place and make a contrast to the inevitable individual scale of the multiple tables and booths. Besides the letters, stripes make old-fashioned borders, which both distinguish and camouflage the junction of wall and ceiling. The color scheme admits a light value on the ceiling and a medium value on the floor. The walls continue the duality by being medium in value at the bottom half (the 5 foot wainscoting) and light in value above. The colors are secondary and cheerful but masculine in character. The colors on the sign outside are unrelated to those inside because the outside is different from the inside. They are primary and more vivid.

Since this restaurant is composed of two houses, its new façade is a juxtaposition of one and two elements—again a play in dualities. The old row houses, which have an almost continuous cornice, are identical in the upper stories. Duality is minimized by painting these stories an allover dark, neutral gray. A duality is necessarily emphasized on the ground floor by the central structural pier between large openings. The face of the wall is left undisturbed except for the applied dark gray. Within the frames of the two openings a contrastingly new and varied wall treatment—concave on the entrance side, convex on the other—occurs. These differences further emphasize the duality on the ground floor of the façade.

But it is the porcelain-enameled sign at the level of the second floor that boldly concludes the simultaneous play of duality and unity, derived from the existing composition of the building. In its extension across the whole front the sign encourages unity; yet in its division of colors—blue on the right and yellow on the left—it points up the duality of the original building. In the continuity of the punched letters on white plastic, continuity across is reestablished.

The cup similarly attracts the eye by being unifying and disrupting at once. With it the sign evolves from two

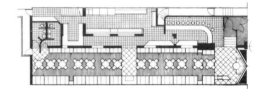

284

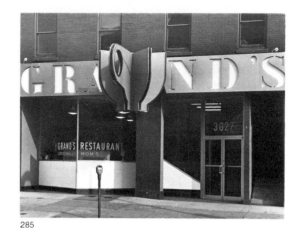

285

286

dimensions to three, so that it can be seen by pedestrians as they approach parallel to the façade, in contrast to the flat part of the sign which can be seen at a distance. The cup's leaves, as the central transition between the blue and yellow sides, are alternately blue and yellow and change visually as you move past them. At night the letters become translucent white light, and the cup was to have been outlined in neon before the sign was modified by the owners. The bold scale of the letters is appropriate to their advertising function. And the division of the word plays up the duality and catches the eye reluctant to read advertisements.

In the end we were one-upped by the owners whose changes made a parody of our parody.

7. Meiss House Projects, Princeton, N.J., Venturi and Short, 1962. (289–295)

The site for this house in Princeton was a very large corner lot, flat and facing south toward the back with a view onto an old stable and a field of the Institute for Advanced Studies. It contained some patches of young trees and a row of old apple trees. The program called for a large study for the professor, easily accessible from the front door and from his small bedroom; plenty of particularized storage space, and an indoor swimming pool, in addition to the usual rooms in a medium-sized house. The clients liked privacy and plenty of sun inside.

The composition of Scheme One is a duality. From the front it superimposes a long gable-roofed element on the back of a shed-roofed one. Essentially, the front zone contains entrances, circulation, storage, services, and swimming pool, and it shields the back element, which contains the rooms for living. Upstairs in the front are two guest rooms, one of which the wife would also use as an office. The violent meeting of these independent roof forms seen from the front allows various clerestory windows for the shed-roofed back zone.

The duality is resolved by the perimeter, especially severe at the sides, which contains the two elements and contributes unity to the composition at this level. Also, in plan the back wall looking onto the long terrace is particularly complex in window indentations—which modify the sunlight or affect the interior space—in contrast with the severe front wall. The front wall's irregular window openings balance the otherwise over-symmetrical pediment façade. The wall in front, a third superimposed element, and the garage, slanted in plan to suggest an auto court, imply enclosure.

The clients did not like Scheme One because they thought a linear plan precluded privacy outside in the back. Therefore the essentially L-shaped plan evolved into a similarly sunny and particularly complex character in the back walls, which contrasted with the severe, closed character of the front walls of the L. However, the complex roofs here meld into each other rather than abut violently. The upstairs bedrooms, windows, and balcony are carved within these roofs so as not to break their continuity with the dormers. But the shed-roof, entrance-front space does abut the other roofs, and the resultant clerestory window hints from the front at the complexity in the back. The fenced service yard, pointed at the end, emphasizes the wall-like protective function on the front or outside perimeter of the L. The clients didn't like this scheme either.

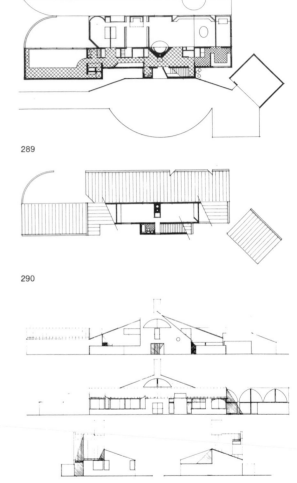

289

290

291

292

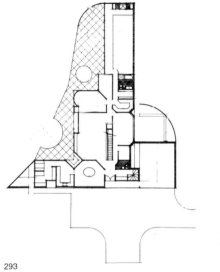

293

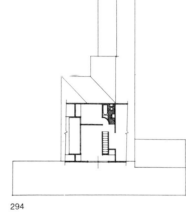

294

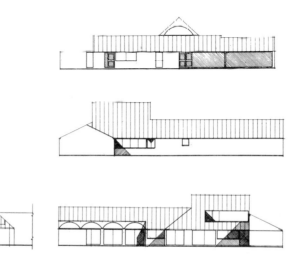

295

8. Guild House, Friends Housing for the Elderly, Philadelphia, Venturi and Rauch, Cope and Lippincott, Associated Architects, 1960–1963. (296–304)

The program required 91 apartments of varying types with a common recreation room, to house elderly people who want to remain in their old neighborhood. Local zoning limited the building height to six stories.

The small urban site faces south on Spring Garden Street. The interior program suggested a maximum of apartments facing south, southeast, and southwest for light and for the interesting activity of the street—yet the urban character of the street suggested a building that would not be an independent pavilion, but instead would recognize the spatial demands of the street in front. This results in a building inflected in shape, whose front is different from its back. The front façade is separated from the back at its top ends where the common room terraces occur in order to emphasize the vestigial role of the street façade. The contrastingly intricate side façades, more sensitive to interior than exterior spatial demands in their exact configurations, accommodate the need for maximum southeast and southwest light, views, and garden space below.

The interior spaces are defined by intricate mazes of walls, which accommodate the very complex and varied program of an apartment house (as opposed to an office building, for example), and the irregular framing allowed by flat plate construction. There is a maximum of interior volume and a minimum of corridor space. The corridor is an irregular and varied residual space rather than a tunnel.

Economy dictated not "advanced" architectural elements, but "conventional" ones. We did not resist this. The dark brown brick walls with double-hung windows recall traditional Philadelphia row houses or even the tenement-like backs of Edwardian apartment houses. Their effect is uncommon, however, because they are subtly proportioned and unusually big. The change in scale of these almost banal elements contributes an expression of tension and a quality to these façades, which now read as both conventional and unconventional forms at the same time.

The big round exposed column at the center of the street façade is polished black granite. It accommodates and emphasizes the exceptional entrance opening on the ground floor, and it contrasts with the white, glazed brick area, which extends to the middle of the second floor on this small section of the street façade. The balcony railings on this floor, like those on the other floors, are perforated steel plate, but here they are painted white rather than black to create a continuity of surface in this area despite the change in material. The central window on the top floor reflects the special spatial configuration of the common room inside and relates to the entrance below, increasing the scale of the building on the street and at the entrance. Its arched shape also permits a very big opening to penetrate the wall and yet remain a hole in a wall rather than a void in a frame. The television antenna atop this axis and beyond the otherwise constant height line of the building strengthens this axis of scale-change in the zone of the central façade, and expresses a kind of monumentality similar to that at the entrance at Anet. The antenna, with its anodized gold surface, can be interpreted two ways: abstractly, as sculpture in the manner of Lippold, and as a symbol of the aged, who spend so much time looking at T.V.

The ornamental line created by a row of white bricks contradictorily intersects the row of upper windows, but it terminates the otherwise plain façade. With the area of white glazed bricks on the front below, it also sets up a new and larger scale of three stories, juxtaposed on the other smaller scale of six stories demarked by the layers of windows.

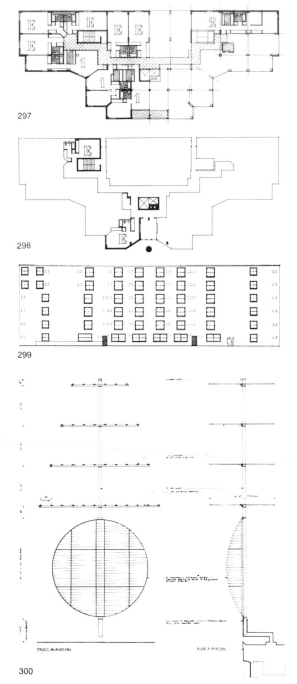

297

298

299

300

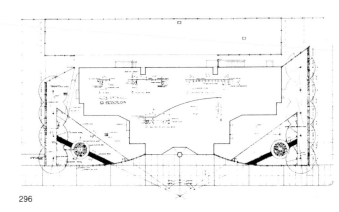

296

301

303

302

304

9. Residence in Chestnut Hill, Pa., Venturi and Rauch, 1962. (305–316)

This building recognizes complexities and contradictions: it is both complex and simple, open and closed, big and little; some of its elements are good on one level and bad on another; its order accommodates the generic elements of the house in general, and the circumstantial elements of a house in particular. It achieves the difficult unity of a medium number of diverse parts rather than the easy unity of few or many motival parts.

The inside spaces, as represented in plan and section, are complex and distorted in their shapes and interrelationships. They correspond to the complexities inherent in the domestic program as well as to some whimsies not inappropriate to an individual house. On the other hand, the outside form—as represented by the parapeted wall and the gable roof which enclose these complexities and distortions—is simple and consistent: it represents this house's public scale. The front, in its conventional combinations of door, windows, chimney and gable, creates an almost symbolic image of a house.

The contradiction between inside and outside, however, is not total: inside, the plan as a whole reflects the symmetrical consistency of the outside; outside, the perforations in the elevations reflect the circumstantial distortions within. Concerning the inside, the plan is originally symmetrical with a central vertical core from which radiate two almost symmetrical diagonal walls that separate two end spaces in front from a major central space in back. This almost Palladian rigidity and symmetry is distorted, however, to accommodate to the particular needs of the spaces: the kitchen on the right, for instance, varies from the bedroom on the left.

A more violent kind of accommodation occurs within the central core itself. Two vertical elements—the fireplace-chimney and the stair—compete, as it were, for central position. And each of these elements, one essentially solid, the other essentially void, compromises in its shape and position—that is, inflects toward the other to make a unity of the duality of the central core they constitute. On one side the fireplace distorts in shape and moves over a little, as does its chimney; on the other side the stair suddenly constricts its width and distorts its path because of the chimney.

This core dominates as the center of the composition at this level; but at the level of its base, it is a residual element dominated itself by the spaces around it. On the living room side its shape is rectangular, and parallel to the important rectangular order of the important space there. Toward the front it is shaped by a diagonal wall accommodating to the also important and unique directional needs of the entrance space in its transition from big outer opening to inner entrance doors. The entrance space also competes for center position here. The stair, considered as an element alone in its awkward residual space, is bad; in relation to its position in a hierarchy of uses and spaces, however, it is a fragment appropriately accommodating to a complex and contradictory whole and as such it is good. From still another point of view its shape is not awkward: at the bottom the stair is a place to sit, as well as ascend, and put objects later to be taken upstairs. And this stair, like those in Shingle Style houses, also wants to be bigger at its base to accommodate to the bigger scale of the first floor. The little "nowhere stair" from the second floor similarly accommodates awkwardly to its residual core space: on one level, it goes nowhere and is whimsical; at another level, it is like a ladder against a wall from which to wash the high window and paint the clerestory. The change in scale of the stair on this floor further contrasts with that change of scale in the other direction at the bottom.

The architectural complexities and distortions inside are reflected on the outside. The varying locations and sizes and shapes of the windows and perforations on the outside walls, as well as the off-center location of the chimney, contradict the overall symmetry of the outside form: the windows are balanced on each side of the dominating entrance opening and chimney-clerestory element in the front, and the lunette window in the back, but they are asymmetrical. The protrusions above and beyond the rigid outside walls also reflect the complexity inside. The walls in front and back are parapeted to emphasize their role as screens behind which these inner intricacies can protrude. Indentations of the windows and porch on the sides at all but one of the corners, increase the screenlike quality of the front and back walls in the same way as the parapets do at their tops.

When I called this house both open and closed as well as simple and complex, I was referring to these contradictory characteristics of the outside walls. First, their parapets

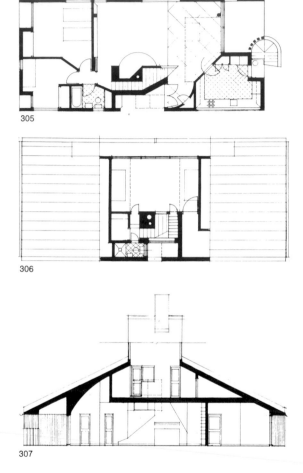

305

306

307

along with the wall of the upper terrace in the back, emphasize horizontal enclosure yet permit an expression of openness behind them at the upper terrace, and above them at the chimney-clerestory protrusion. Second, the consistent shape of the walls in plan emphasizes rigid enclosure, yet the big openings, often precariously close to the corners contradict the expression of enclosure. This method of walls—layered for enclosure, yet punctured for openness—occurs vividly at the front center, where the outside wall is superimposed upon the two other walls housing the stair. Each of these three layers juxtaposes openings of differing size and position. Here is layered space rather than inter-penetrated space.

The house is big as well as little, by which I mean that it is a little house with big scale. Inside the elements are big: the fireplace is "too big" and the mantel "too high" for the size of the room; doors are wide, the chair rail high. Another manifestation of big scale inside is a minimum of subdivisions of space—also for the sake of economy, the plan minimizes purely circulation space. Outside the manifestations of big scale are the main elements, which are big and few in number and central or symmetrical in position, as well as the simplicity and consistency of the form and silhouette of the whole, which I have already described. In back the lunette window is big and dominating in its shape and position. In front the entrance loggia is wide, high, and central. Its big scale is emphasized by its contrast with the other doors, smaller in size yet similar in shape; by its shallowness for its size; and by the expedient position of the inner entrance behind it. The applied wood moulding over the door increases its scale, too. The dado increases the scale of the building all around because it is higher than you expect it to be. These mouldings affect the scale in another way also: they make the stucco walls even more abstract, and the scale, usually implied by the nature of materials, more ambiguous or noncommital.

The main reason for the large scale is to counterbalance the complexity. Complexity in combination with small scale in small buildings means busyness. Like the other organized complexities here, the big scale in the small building achieves tension rather than nervousness—a tension appropriate for this kind of architecture.

The setting of the house is a flat, open, interior site, enclosed at its boundaries by trees and fences. The house sits near the middle, like a pavilion, with no planting at all

308

309

310

near it. The driveway axis perpendicular to the middle of the house is distorted in its position by the circumstantial location of a sewer main at the curb of the street.

The abstract composition of this building almost equally combines rectangular, diagonal, and curving elements. The rectangles relate to the just dominant order of the spaces in plan and section. The diagonals relate to directional space at the entrance, to particular relationships of the directional and nondirectional spaces within the rigid enclosure on the first floor, and to the enclosing and water-shedding function of the roof. The curves relate to the directional-spatial needs at the entry and outside stair; to spatial-expressive needs in section in the dining room ceiling, which is contradictory to the outside slope of the roof; and to the symbolism of the entrance and its big scale, which is produced by the moulding on the front elevation. The exceptional point in the plan refers to the expedient column support, which contrasts with the otherwise wall-bearing structure of the whole. These complex combinations do not achieve the easy harmony of a few motival parts based on exclusion—based, that is, on "less is more." Instead they achieve the difficult unity of a medium number of diverse parts based on inclusion and on acknowledgement of the diversity of experience.

311

312

314

313

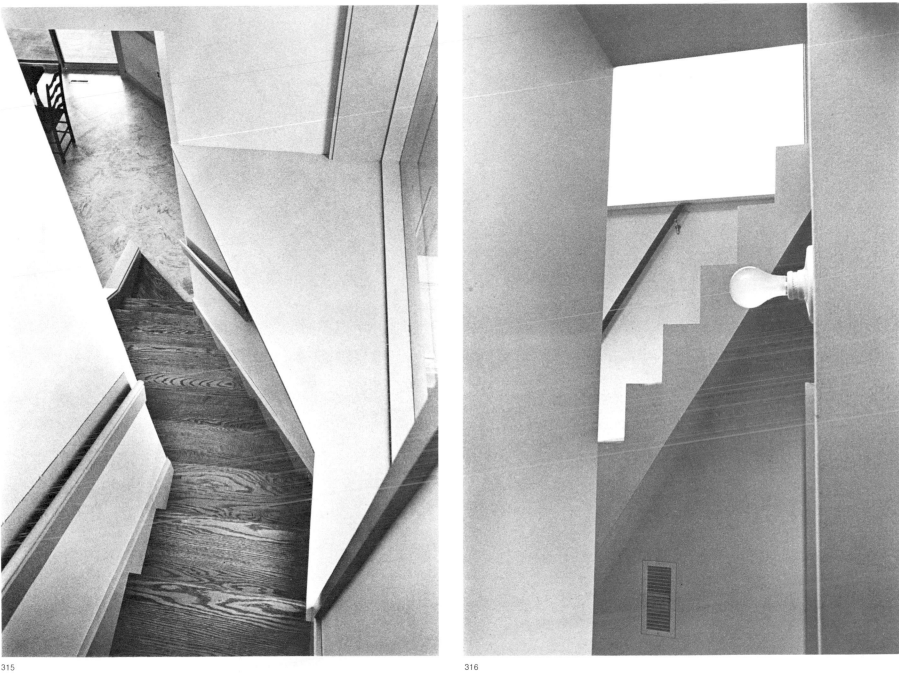

315

316

10. Fountain Competition, Fairmount Park Association, Philadelphia, Venturi and Rauch, Denise Scott Brown, 1964. (317–322)

This fountain was to be located within the open city block that terminates the Benjamin Franklin Parkway in front of City Hall. The block is common to the gridiron plan of the center of the city and is surrounded by streets with plenty of local traffic. Beyond it, except along the through-axis to the Parkway, looms a jumble of high office buildings. The interior of the almost square block contains an existing round pavilion called the Information Center. The landscaping and paving layout, including the 90 foot diameter basin for the fountain itself, were elements established by the competition program. The Benjamin Franklin Parkway is a boulevard whose axis is about a mile in length, and diagonal to and intersecting with the normal gridiron plan of the city. It connects City Hall with the Art Museum and Fairmount Park beyond.

In the other direction it can also be considered an extension of the park into the center of the city because its green trees make a continuity with the park itself, and it is also under legal jurisdiction of the Fairmount Park Commission. The Parkway acts as an important arterial approach to the center of the city and focuses on the dominant form of City Hall—the field against which the fountain is to be viewed. City Hall is light in color, large in size and scale, and ornate in pattern and silhouette. These characteristics of space, form, scale, and circulation, which make up the context of the fountain, largely determine its form.

The form is big and bold so that it will read against its background of big buildings and amorphous space, and also from the relatively long distance up the Parkway. Its plastic shape, curving silhouette, and plain surface also contrast boldly with the intricate rectangular patterns of the buildings around, although they are analogous to some of the mansard roof shapes on City Hall. This was not meant to be an intricate Baroque fountain to be read only close-up, or from a car stalled in traffic.

But the action of the water itself, as well as the context of the surroundings, determines the particularities of the sculpture's form. The scale of the water's action matches that of the sculpture: the central jet is 60 feet high and relates to the scale as well as to the axis of the Parkway. Its

constant stream is shielded from the prevailing wind by the concave, inner surface of the sculptural form. It is exposed only toward the Parkway, and it is set off by the dark background of the enclosure. From most parts of the plaza only the reverberations of the great jet within the misty and mossy artificial grotto are evident. The large aluminum shield corresponds to little glass shields that protect the flame from drafts in some kinds of old-fashioned candelabra.

If the inner surface of the sculpture is concave to accommodate to the large-scale water action there, the outer surface is convex to accommodate to the small-scale water action outside. This consists of a constant sheet of water issuing from a weir near the top of the surface and continuously dripping from its lower edge into the pool. The legend HERE BEGINS FAIRMOUNT PARK is glimpsed through a screen of droplets. This waterfall, with the polished, elongated letters on the sloping surface of the base behind, relates to the scale of the individual walking around the immediate plaza and is designed to engage his interest.

Lettering is traditional on monuments. The legend designates the dramatic penetration of the biggest urban park in the world into the heart of the city. When the legend is read from the front elevation it appears to say PARK HERE, not inappropriately for a monument over an underground parking lot.

The central jet is spotlighted by quartz lamps recessed in the base. In the winter, when the jet is inactive, incandescent lamps with amber lenses flood the angular maze of the in-between core structure with yellow light. The central space is then dark. The angled base is floodlighted by amber-lensed incandescent lamps. This continuous band contrasts with the looming dark body above, and at close range it illuminates the legend.

The material is aluminum to lighten the weight on the spans of the garage below. Its surface is sandblasted to promote a dark, mat, warm gray finish. The sheets are welded, but the joints are not ground smooth. The structure is a skin structure with stacked, bent-plates inside (themselves bent into "Z" sections), which act both as spacers between the contradictory inside and outside silhouettes and as integral bracing, like the inner corrugations of laminated cardboard box sections. The geometry of the inner plates is angular, and it contacts the curvilinear surfaces of the outer plates at welded points. This airy poché is exposed at the openings of the enclosure, back and front. A

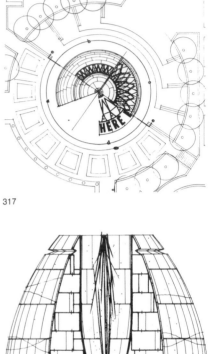

317

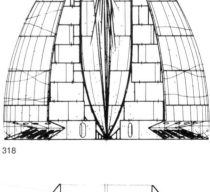

318

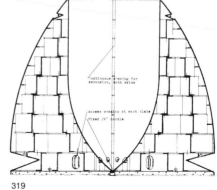

319

320

321

322

series of vertical manholes for maintenance are located in the lower plates. These contribute a scale that contrasts with the monumental scale of the whole.

This fountain is big and little in scale, sculptural and architectural in structure, analogous and contrasting in its context, directional and nondirectional, curvilinear and angular in its form, it was designed from the inside out and from the outside in.

11. Three Buildings for a Town in Ohio, Venturi and Rauch, 1965. (323–347)

The three buildings for a town in Ohio are a town hall, a Y.M.C.A., and a public library, or rather an extensive addition to one. These buildings relate to each other urbanistically and to the center of the town they are a part of. They are a part of the beginning stage as well, of a larger plan for the renewal of the center of the town which is the design responsibility of planning consultants whom we are working under.

The town hall: the town hall is like a Roman temple in its general proportions, and also because it is free-standing, but—in contrast with a Greek temple—a directional building whose front is more important than its back. What corresponds to the base, the giant columns and the pediment of the porch of the temple is, in this city hall, the partially disengaged wall in front with its giant arched opening superimposed on the three-storied wall beyond. I like Louis Sullivan's use of the giant arch to give image, unity, and monumental scale to some of his late banks which are important but small buildings on the main streets of mid-Western towns. The change in size and scale in the front of the town hall is analogous also to the false fronts of western towns, and for the same reason: to acknowledge the urban spatial demands of the street. But this building has two settings at once. Besides its position as an important if smallish, building along Main Street, it also sits at the end of the central plaza across Main Street where it terminates the longitudinal axis of the plaza. Also, to the observer on Main Street the building rests right on the ground with its first floor always visible as an integral base; from within the plaza which is lower than Main Street, however, the first floor is obscured in perspective by the elevation and depth of the street immediately in front of it and by the ramped steps leading up which form another kind of base for the building. In this context the arch of the façade appears to spring directly from a different and greater-scaled base. The same building in different contexts is read in different ways.

The contradiction in scale and character between the front and back of this building derives from the particular program inside as well as the urban setting outside. The dichotomy in the program of a town hall between the monumental spaces for the mayor and the council on one hand, and the routine offices for the administrative departments on the other hand are often explicitly articulated into a pavilion for the former connected with an office slab for the latter, a composition based on the Pavillon Suisse or perhaps the Armée du Salut. (Another approach perhaps is to base the town hall on another composition of Le Corbusier's, La Tourette, where the composition looks incomplete but is essentially closed.) But this scheme for a small town hall accommodates these two kinds of spaces within a relatively simple enclosure for the sake of scale and economy. (The mayor said he wanted "a sensible, square, masonry building.") The monumental and more ceremonial rooms up front are unique and static—with the growth of the town only a few more council members will ever be added and there will never be more than one mayor—while the small scale, but relatively extensive and flexible office spaces behind are expansible: you can add on to the back. This is an open-ended building in the back because bureaucracy is always growing. Between the front and the back is a common zone for vertical circulation and services. The first floor contains police facilities in the back and the main entrance in the front. It is assumed that the public will frequent less and less a town hall so that the bill-paying and information areas are not on the ground floor. The small repetitive windows toward the back and the greater height of the buttressed front façade from the side reflect further these interior variations of function. The structure is concrete bearing wall forming parallel or perpendicular zones spanned by concrete joists. In the back zone there is an interior column in the center to facilitate flexibility within the bearing walls. The wide corridor or gallery which is anticipated here is appropriate for an office area with wider public use. Since the bearing walls are concrete, the openings can be very big. The surface material is dark brick similar to but not matching the existing big factory in the center of the town. The front screen wall, however, is faced with very thin white marble slabs to reemphasize the contrast between the front and the back. On the front also, the juxtaposition of the big arched opening on the smaller windows of the wall behind changes to the same plane at the council chamber on the third floor. The window here matches the big scale of the front screen: it consists of one piece of glass about 28 by 30 feet. The enormous flag is perpendicular to the street so that it reads from up the street like a commercial sign.

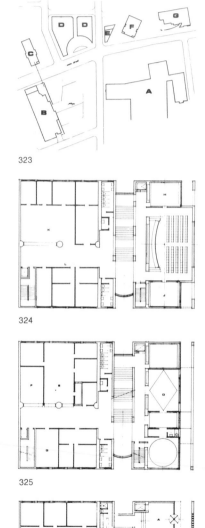

323

324

325

326

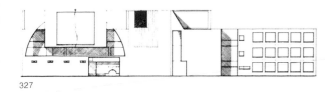

327

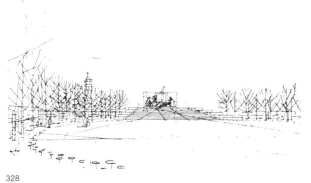

328

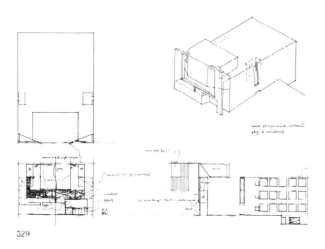

329

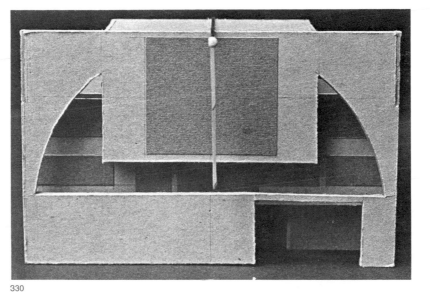

330

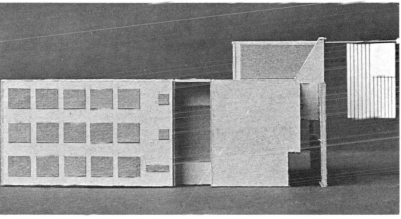

331

The Y.M.C.A.: this building follows closely the conventional, rather explicit, and complex recommendations for the interior program of a Y.M.C.A. of this size. Our variations might include the zoning of the athletic spaces behind, the social spaces up front, the elevation above the basement level of the extensive locker rooms, and some characteristics which come from the sloping site along the length of the building and the need for entrances in the back from the parking and from the anticipated shopping area behind, as well as in the front from the plaza. But the position of the building along the side of the plaza and opposite the existing, dominating factory had the greatest effect on the outside expression of the building.

This building had to be big in scale to complement and not be overpowered by the factory opposite. This was accomplished by the size, number, and relationship of the elements of the front façade. The openings in the wall were few and big to increase the scale. The relationship of the openings which are the dominant elements of the façade make up a relatively constant rhythm without focus in the center or emphasis at the terminations. This characteristic also gives greater unity and scale to the building. In its overall composition it does not create a beginning, middle, and end which make up three things; it is just one continuous thing resulting from the constant, even boring, rhythm. In this way it can compete with the factory opposite which is bigger as a whole but smaller in its individual parts. And it is appropriately secondary to the smaller city hall on another side of the plaza. The front façade, like that of the city hall, is "false"—a free-standing wall—contradictory in relation to the interior space. The almost constant rhythm of grid-opening is played against the smaller and more irregular rhythms of the two-story building-proper behind. A contrapuntal juxtaposition contrasts the "boredom" of the false façade with the "chaos" of the back façade which reflects the interior circumstantial complexities. The front wall contains a buffer zone between building and plaza for skaters in the winter on the left side, and an outdoor niche with fireplace for them on the right where it becomes a retaining wall, and also a great ramp on axis with the existing church on Main Street. The structure is concrete bearing wall, which allows big openings close together—it is indeed, a quasi-frame construction. The dark face brick relates to the existing factory and increases the unity of the plaza and the center of the town.

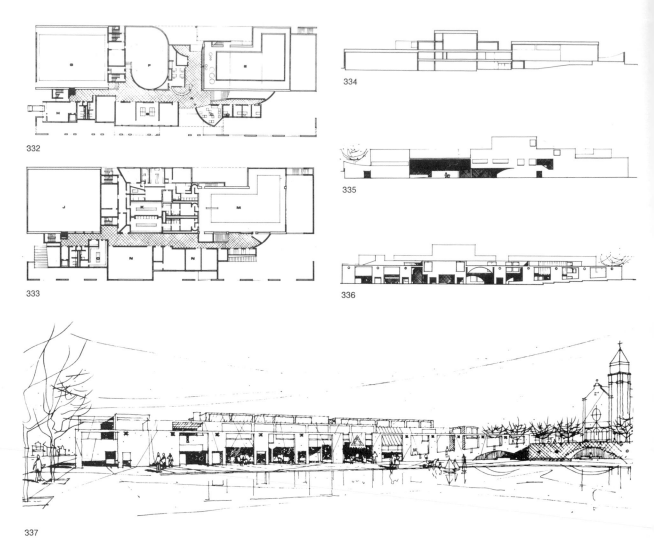

332

333

334

335

336

337

126

338

341

339

340

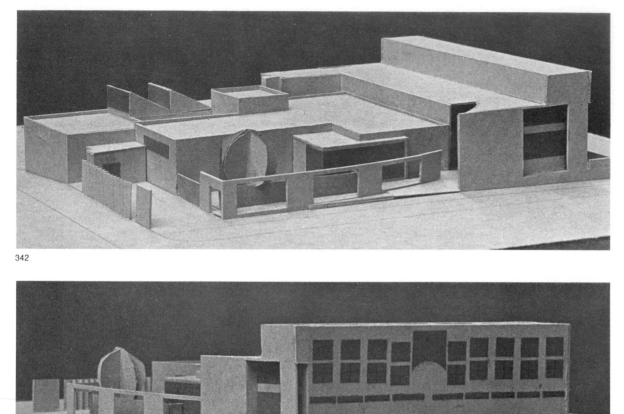

342

343

344

345

346

347

The library addition: the interior program is almost
entirely conventional. Our approach was to wrap around
rather than add to, the existing buff brick building with
new interior spaces on the back and the north side and with
a new detached wall in front which contains a court in its
residual space. The old building is covered over but modified as little as possible for economy. The wraparound wall,
in its big scale and dark brick material increases the unity
of Main Street. Through the big, grilled openings in the
front outer wall is glimpsed the older, lighter, small-scale
building so that its architecture is respected. From close-up
the new is juxtaposed upon the old.

12. Copley Square Competition, Venturi and Rauch, Gerod Clark and Arthur Jones, 1966. (348–350)

For a large open space in an American city Copley Square in Boston is quite contained—on the south by the hotel, on the west by the Public Library, at the northwest corner by the new Old South Church and by the row of commercial buildings on the north. But the open corner toward the southwest where the diagonal Huntington Avenue is to be terminated, and the leaking corner toward the southeast between Trinity Church and Copley Plaza tend to weaken the sense of enclosure. And toward the east the space is enclosed ambiguously by Trinity Church itself which tends to sit in the square rather than along it. The varying heights, rhythms and scales of these buildings as well as the streets which separate them from the center of the space, further diminish the spatial unity of the existing square.

The rules of the competition confined the area to be designed within the block defined by the interior sidewalks of the three streets and the diagonal sidewalk along the northwest side of Trinity Church; of course, we could not change nor anticipate change in any of the disparate buildings around the space.

So we made a non-piazza; we filled up the space to define the space.

We filled it with non-dense matter, a consistent but rich grid of trees. These trees are too far apart to make a traditional bosque, yet too dense to be read as discreet elements. When you walk among them they are far enough apart to filter light with variety and to veil the church tantalizingly (you have to struggle to see the great façade) but from without, along the streets, they are a rigid form which defines the space and identifies the place. Their form as a whole, however (unlike our fountain project for Philadelphia in a different kind of context), is not a sculptural form sitting *in* a space because that would compete with Trinity Church. It is an overall, three-dimensional repetitive pattern without a climax, separated from the surroundings by the border of streets, and in contrast with Trinity Church which at one level of focus is accent enough in the whole composition. In the context of the "boring" consistent grid inside the square the chaotic buildings to the north become "interesting" and vital elements of the composition.

Besides the mosaic of trees and tall lampposts, there is at a lower level, a grid-order made up of stepped mounds about four feet high between walkways. This grid reflects in miniature the gridiron pattern of the part of Boston surrounding Copley Square. It imitates the hierarchy of streets, big, little and medium found in the real city. Like the real gridiron city, it contains diagonal "avenues" which facilitate circulation and whose juxtaposition creates exceptional, residual blocks.

Within the blocks of the lower grid is another pattern of benches, trash cans and drains in phase with the grid of trees and lampposts. This furniture, like the lampposts, is composed of conventional elements given new value by their new context. These "vulgar" elements are not specially designed; they are only thoughtfully chosen. (Compare these aluminum lampposts with the tastefully exotic bronze-like, anodized aluminum ones around the green in New Haven.) Materials are similarly plain except for the precious brick areas under the benches which make more vivid the banality of the blacktop walkways and the pre-cast concrete of the stepped block sections, gutters and drains. There is grass only on top of the blocks where it will receive a minimum of wear. Rows of flowers atop the blocks border the avenues to extend the width of the avenues visually. Where the blocks are cut through, the check walls have very bold inscriptions of nursery rhymes, etc., cast into the concrete to interest children who cannot see over the blocks.

The grid of trees, lampposts and street furniture and that of the hierarchy of streets are out of phase with each other along the north-south axes. These slight irregularities of rhythms contrast with the violent irregularities which come from the juxtapositions of the diagonal avenues upon the gridiron pattern of the streets which are manifest as I have said, in the residual, fragmentary blocks, triangular and polygonal in shape. Indeed, because of these contrapuntal juxtapositions of diagonals and the truncations at the borders almost no typical or pure blocks remain. And of these, two are made exceptional. One block is reversed in section: that is, depressed exactly in the manner that the typical ones are elevated in order to make a little piazza to sit in in contrast with the typical walks you sit along; the other is level to contain a miniature replica of Trinity Church. The fragmentary blocks along the north side, gouged out with niches to sit in, are further exceptions.

This play of exceptions to the order, slight or violent, creates tensions within the grid that contradict the boringness of the pattern. But there is a play of scale too which creates within the pattern a kind of monumentality as well as ambiguity and tension. It involves a particular relationship of size and proportion. The juxtapositions of streets of different size on the grid results in blocks of different size but similar proportion, and a combination of trees, one big and two little, within the grid pattern, makes for a similar relationship of elements of different size but same proportion. (This idea is anathema to orthodox Modern architects who hold that change in size means change in proportion to reflect exclusively a structural basis for form and proportion. On the other hand Jasper Johns in his paintings juxtaposes conventionally proportioned flags which are big, little and medium in size.) The species of trees was chosen with this in mind: the form of the mature Plane tree, about 60 feet in height, has a similar proportion to that of the mature Scholar tree, about 25 feet high. The element which most vividly exemplifies this idea is the replica in cast concrete of Trinity Church in front of Trinity Church.

There is a reason for this little replica and that of the gridiron "streets" too—a reason other than those reasons already mentioned effecting ambiguity, tension, scale and monumentality: the miniature imitation is a means for explaining to a person the whole which he is in but cannot see all of. To reassure the individual by making the whole comprehensible in this way within a part is to contribute a sense of unity to a complex urban whole. This kind of imitation in miniature involves as well an imitation of one aspect of life. To condense experience and make it more vivid, to pretend, that is, is a characteristic of play: children play house. Adults play Monopoly. In this square it is a simulation of urban circulation and space. The little church is play sculpture for children too.

Another characteristic of play which is lacking in Modern, architect-designed urban spaces is the opportunity for choice and improvisation: that is, for people to use the same spaces in many different ways including ways the spaces are not explicitly designed for. The grid, whether in the form and scale of the town plan or countryside of the American mid-west or the columned interiors of a mosque in Cairo or Cordova, allows for improvisation and variety of use. In a Victorian mansion there are probably more ways of using the eventful stairway than of walking

through and sitting in a typical modern square. When form follows function explicitly, the opportunities for implicit functions decrease. There are probably more ways to use this square which is "just a grid" than there are to use those which are interesting, sensitive and human. And more important, there are more ways to *see* it. It is like the intricate pattern of a plaid fabric. From a distance it is an overall repetitive pattern—from a great distance, indeed, it is a plain blur—but close up it is intricate, varied and rich in pattern, texture, scale and color. (In this spatial plaid there is the added dimension I have mentioned, of slight and violent exceptions.) It is a question of focus: as one moves around and through the composition, he can focus on different things and relationships in different ways. There are opportunities to see the same thing in different ways, the old thing in new ways. As there is not a single, constant accent—a fountain, reflecting pool nor the great church itself, for instance, neither is there a single static focus when you move within and around the square. There is the opportunity for a variety of focuses, or rather for changing focus. The main paradox of this design is that the boring pattern is interesting.

Violent juxtapositions of blurred and sharp focuses come from levels of relationships which relate more or less to the whole, or in complex compositions, to wholes within wholes. These changing relationships within complex wholes make for complex kinds of unity some of whose immediate interior relationships involve distinct disunity. Not all the relationships are always all right. I think "relating" buildings is an eighth crutch of Modern architecture which Philip Johnson might have included. Buildings like Trinity Church and the Boston Public Library don't have to be "related" in easy and obvious ways. And they shouldn't be because their relationships cannot be just immediate to the interior setting of the square, but to greater wholes outside themselves and their immediate setting. Our little grid from a distance (like the plaid pattern) is a big blur because of its consistency at this level of focus: it does not always relate close-up and in detail therefore to the fine buildings around it. Richardson and McKim, Mead and White don't need that kind of explicit homage.

Another crutch of Modern architecture is the piazza compulsion derived from our justifiable love of Italian towns. But the open piazza is seldom appropriate for an American city today except as a convenience for pedestrians

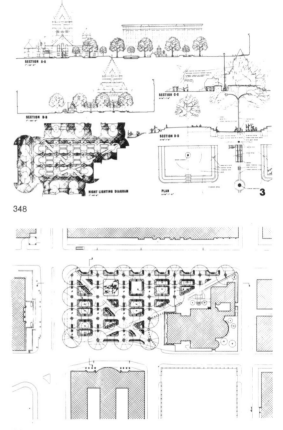

348

349

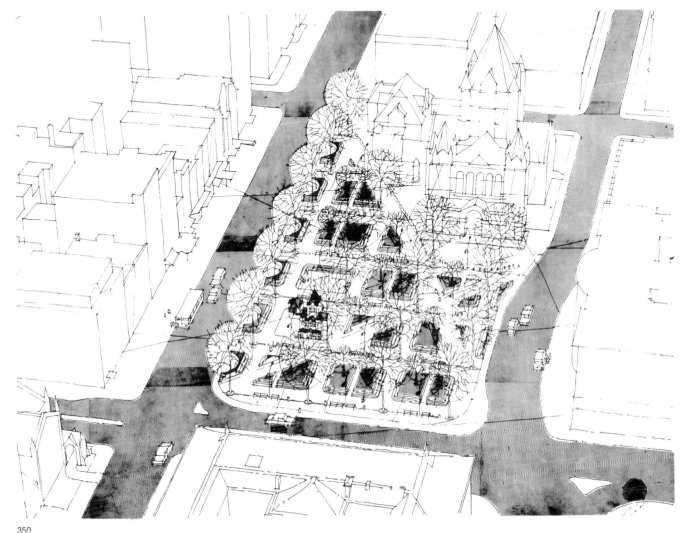

350

for diagonal short-cuts. The piazza, in fact, is "un-American." Americans feel uncomfortable sitting in a square: they should be working at the office or home with the family looking at television. Chores around the house or the weekend drive have replaced the passeggiata. The traditional piazza is for collective use as well as individual use, and public ceremonies involving crowds are even harder to imagine in Copley Square than passeggiate. Our square therefore is not an open space to accommodate non-existing crowds (empty piazzas are intriguing only in early de Chiricos), but to accommodate the individual who comfortably walks through the maze and sits along the "streets" rather than in a "piazza." We are in the habit of thinking that open space is precious in the city. It is not. Except in Manhattan perhaps, our cities have too much open space in the ubiquitous parking lots, in the not-so-temporary deserts created by Urban Renewal and in the amorphous suburbs around.

1   T. S. Eliot: *Selected Essays, 1917–1932,* Harcourt, Brace and Co., New York, 1932; p. 18.
2   *Ibid.;* pp. 3–4.
3   Aldo van Eyck: in *Architectural Design 12,* vol. XXXII, December 1962; p. 560.
4   Henry-Russell Hitchcock: in *Perspecta 6, The Yale Architectural Journal,* New Haven, 1960; p. 2.
5   *Ibid.;* p. 3.
6   Robert L. Geddes: in *The Philadelphia Evening Bulletin.* February 2, 1965; p. 40.
7   Sir John Summerson: *Heavenly Mansions,* W. W. Norton and Co., Inc., New York, 1963; p. 197.
8   *Ibid.;* p. 200.
9   David Jones: *Epoch and Artist,* Chilmark Press, Inc., New York, 1959; p. 12.
10 Kenzo Tange: in *Documents of Modern Architecture,* Jurgen Joedicke, ed., Universe Books, Inc., New York, 1961; p. 170.
11 Frank Lloyd Wright: in *An American Architecture,* Edgar Kaufmann, ed., Horizon Press, New York, 1955; p. 207.
12 Le Corbusier: *Towards a New Architecture,* The Architectural Press, London, 1927; p. 31.
13 Christopher Alexander: *Notes on the Synthesis of Form,* Harvard University Press, Cambridge, 1964; p. 4.
14 August Heckscher: *The Public Happiness,* Atheneum Publishers, New York, 1962; p. 102.
15 Paul Rudolph: in *Perspecta 7, The Yale Architectural Journal,* New Haven, 1961; p. 51.
16 Kenneth Burke: *Permanence and Change,* Hermes Publications, Los Altos, 1954; p. 107.
17 Eliot, *op. cit.;* p. 96.
18 T. S. Eliot: *Use of Poetry and Use of Criticism,* Harvard University Press, Cambridge, 1933; p. 146.
19 Eliot: *Selected Essays, 1917–1932, op. cit.;* p. 243.
20 *Ibid.;* p. 98.
21 Cleanth Brooks: *The Well Wrought Urn,* Harcourt, Brace and World, Inc., New York, 1947; pp 212–214.
22 Stanley Edgar Hyman: *The Armed Vision,* Vintage Books, Inc., New York, 1955; p. 237.
23 *Ibid.;* p. 240.
24 William Empson: *Seven Types of Ambiguity,* Meridian Books, Inc., New York, 1955; p. 174.
25 Hyman, *op. cit.;* p. 238.
26 Brooks, *op. cit.;* p. 81.
27 Wylie Sypher: *Four Stages of Renaissance Style,* Doubleday and Co., Inc., Garden City, 1955; p. 124.
28 Frank Lloyd Wright: *An Autobiography,* Duell, Sloan and Pearce, New York, 1943; p. 148.
29 Eliot: *Selected Essays, 1917–1932, op. cit.;* p. 185.
30 Brooks, *op. cit.;* p. 7.

31 Burke, *op. cit.;* p. 69.
32 Alan R. Solomon: *Jasper Johns,* The Jewish Museum, New York, 1964; p. 5.
33 James S. Ackerman: *The Architecture of Michelangelo,* A. Zwemmer, Ltd., London, 1961; p. 139.
34 Siegfried Giedion: *Space, Time and Architecture,* Harvard University Press, Cambridge, 1963; p. 565.
35 Eliel Saarinen: *Search for Form,* Reinhold Publishing Corp., New York, 1948; p. 254.
36 Van Eyck, *op. cit.;* p. 602.
37 Frank Lloyd Wright: *Modern Architecture,* Princeton University Press, Princeton, 1931. (front end paper)
38 Horatio Greenough: in *Roots of Contemporary American Architecture,* Lewis Mumford, ed., Grove Press, Inc., New York, 1959; p. 37.
39 Henry David Thoreau: *Walden and Other Writings,* The Modern Library, Random House, New York, 1940; p. 42.
40 Louis H. Sullivan: *Kindergarten Chats,* Wittenborn, Schultz, Inc., New York, 1947; p. 140.
41 *Ibid.;* p. 43.
42 Le Corbusier, *op. cit.;* p. 11.
43 Gyorgy Kepes: *The New Landscape,* P. Theobald, Chicago, 1956; p. 326.
44 Van Eyck, *op. cit.;* p. 600.
45 Heckscher, *op. cit.;* p. 287.
46 Herbert A. Simon: in *Proceedings of the American Philosophical Society,* vol. 106, no. 6, December 12, 1962; p. 468.
47 Arthur Trystan Edwards: *Architectural Style,* Faber and Gwyer, London, 1926; ch. III.
48 Ackerman, *op. cit.;* p. 138.
49 Fumihiko Maki: *Investigations in Collective Form,* Special Publication No. 2, Washington University, St. Louis, 1964; p. 5.
50 Heckscher, *op. cit.;* p. 289.

Photograph Credits

from *Le Corbusier, Oeuvre complète 1946–1952*, 1955. © 1953.

78. Reproduced by permission of George Wittenborn, Inc., New York, from Karl Fleig (editor), *Alvar Aalto*, 1963.
79. Courtesy Louis I. Kahn.
80. The Museum of Modern Art.
81. Hedrich-Blessing.
82. The Museum of Modern Art.
83. The Museum of Modern Art.
84. The Museum of Modern Art.
85. © Ezra Stoller Associates.
86. Charles Brickbauer.
87. Courtesy Peter Blake.
88. Courtesy Peter Blake.
89. Courtesy Peter Blake.
90. © Lucien Hervé, Paris.
91. James L. Dillon & Co., Inc., Philadelphia.
92. Touring Club Italiano, Milan.
93. A. F. Kersting, London.
94. Reproduced by permission of Giulio Einaudi Editore, Turin, from Paolo Portoghesi and Bruno Zevi (editors), *Michelangiolo Architetto*, 1964.
95. Reproduced by permission of Giulio Einaudi Editore, Turin, from Paolo Portoghesi and Bruno Zevi (editors), *Michelangiolo Architetto*, 1964.
96. University News Service, University of Virginia.
97. MAS, Barcelona.
98. Touring Club Italiano, Milan.
99. From Colen Campbell, *Vitruvius Britannicus*, vol. II, London 1717.
100. Collection: Mr. & Mrs. Burton Tremaine, Meriden, Conn.
101. Reproduced by permission of Penguin Books Ltd., Harmondsworth-Middlesex, from Kenneth John Conant, *Carolingian and Romanesque Architecture, 800–1200*, Baltimore 1959.
102. From George William Shel-

don, *Artistic Country-Seats; Types of Recent American Villa and Cottage Architecture, with Instances of Country Clubhouses*, D. Appleton and Company, New York 1886.
103. Photo by Georgina Masson, author of *Italian Villas and Palaces*, Thames and Hudson, London 1959.
104. Photo by John Szarkowski, author of *The Idea of Louis Sullivan*, The University of Minnesota Press, Minneapolis. © 1956 The University of Minnesota.
105. Pix Inc.
106. Archivo Fotografico, Monumenti Musei e Gallerie Pontificie, Vatican City.
107. Reproduced by permission, from *Progressive Architecture*, April 1961.
108. Photo by Martin Hürlimann, author of *Englische Kathedralen*, Atlantis Verlag, Zurich 1956.
109. Courtesy Casa de Portugal. Photo: SNI-YAN.
110. Alinari.
111. Reproduced by permission of Giulio Einaudi Editore, Turin, from Paolo Portoghesi and Bruno Zevi (editors), *Michelangiolo Architetto*, 1964.
112. Chicago Architectural Photo Co.
113. Reproduced by permission of Country Life Ltd., London, from A.S.G. Butler, *The Architecture of Sir Edwin Lutyens*, vol. III, New York 1950. © Country Life.
114. Reproduced by permission, from *Architectural Design*, December 1962.
115. Photo by Martin Hürlimann, author of *Italien*, Atlantis Verlag, Zurich 1959.
116. Bildarchiv Foto Marburg, Marburg/Lahn.

117. Jean Roubier, Paris.
118. Bildarchiv Foto Marburg, Marburg/Lahn.
119. MAS, Barcelona.
120. MAS, Barcelona.
121. Robert Venturi.
122. From Colin Campbell *Vitruvius Britannicus*, vol. III, London 1725.
123. Jean Roubier, Paris.
124. Gebrüder Metz, Tübingen.
125. © Trustees of Sir John Soane's Museum.
126. Alinari.
127. Cunard Line.
128. Alinari.
129. Reproduced by permission of Giulio Einaudi Editore, Turin, from Paolo Portoghesi and Bruno Zevi (editors), *Michelangiolo Architetto*, 1964.
130. Photo by Martin Hürlimann, author of *Italien*, Atlantis Verlag, Zurich 1959.
131. Courtesy of Anton Schroll and Co., Vienna, publisher of Heinrich Decker, *Romanesque Art in Italy*, 1958.
132. Reproduced by permission of Verlag Gebr. Mann, Berlin, from H. Knackfuss, *Didyma*, part I, vol. III, 1940.
133. Reproduced by permission of Country Life Ltd., London, from A.S.G. Butler, *The Architecture of Sir Edwin Lutyens*, vol. I, 1935. © Country Life.
134. The Museum of Modern Art.
135. MAS, Barcelona.
136. California Division of Highways.
137. Alinari.
138. Reproduced by permission of Harry N. Abrams, Inc., New York, from Henry A. Millon and Alfred Frazer, *Key Monuments of the History of Architecture*, 1964.
139. Reproduced by permission of

Henry-Russell Hitchcock from his book *In the Nature of Materials*, Duell, Sloan & Pearce, New York 1942.
140. Archives Nationales, Paris.
141. Archives Nationales, Paris.
142. Touring Club Italiano, Milan.
143. © Trustees of Sir John Soane's Museum.
144. Reproduced by permission of Architectural Book Publishing Co., Inc., New York, from W. Hegemann and E. Peets, *The American Vitruvius*. © 1922 Paul Wenzel and Maurice Krakow.
145. Reproduced by permission of Architectural Book Publishing Co., Inc., New York, from W. Hegemann and E. Peets, *The American Vitruvius*. © 1922 Paul Wenzel and Maurice Krakow.
146. J. B. Piranesi, *Vedute di Roma*, vol. 13. New York Public Library Art Room.
147. Reproduced by permission of Yale University Press, New Haven, from Vincent Scully, *The Shingle Style*, 1955.
148. Reproduced by permission of Architectural Book Publishing Co., Inc., New York, from Katharine Hooker and Myron Hunt, *Farmhouses and Small Provincial Buildings in Southern Italy*, 1925.
149. A. F. Kersting, London.
150. Alinari.
151. The Museum of Modern Art.
152. Theo Frey, Weiningen.
153. Reproduced by permission of George Wittenborn, Inc., New York, from Karl Fleig (editor), *Alvar Aalto*, 1963.
154. Reproduced by permission of Country Life Ltd., London, from H. Avray Tipping and Christopher Hussey, *English Homes, Period IV–Vol. II, The*

Work of Sir John Vanbrugh and His School, 1699–1736, 1928. © Country Life.

155. Reproduced by permission of Propyläen Verlag, Berlin, from Gustav Pauli, *Die Kunst des Klassizismus und der Romantik,* 1925.

156. Alinari.

157. Abraham Guillén, Lima.

158. Archives Photographiques, Caisse Nationale des Monuments Historiques, Paris.

159. Robert Venturi.

160. Bildarchiv Foto Marburg, Marburg/Lahn.

161. © Country Life.

162. Robert Venturi.

163. From Russell Sturgis, *A History of Architecture,* vol. I, The Baker & Taylor Company, New York 1906.

164. Reproduced by permission of Propyläen Verlag, Berlin, from Heinrich Schafer and Walter Andrae, *Die Kunst der Alten Orients,* 1925.

165. Reproduced by permission of Penguin Books Ltd., Harmondsworth-Middlesex, from Rudolf Wittkower, *Art and Architecture in Italy, 1600–1750,* Baltimore 1958.

166. Pierre Devinoy, Paris.

167. Staatlichen Graphischen Sammlung, Munich.

168. Hirmer Verlag, Munich.

169. Reproduced by permission, from *L'Architettura,* June 1964.

170. Alinari.

171. © Trustees of Sir John Soane's Museum.

172. Robert Venturi.

173. Robert Venturi.

174. The Museum of Modern Art.

175. © Ezra Stoller Associates.

176. Ernest Nash, Fototeca Unione, Rome.

177. Reproduced by permission of Penguin Books Ltd., Har-

mondsworth-Middlesex, from Nikolaus Pevsner, *An Outline of European Architecture,* Baltimore 1960.

178. Reproduced by permission of Penguin Books Ltd., Harmondsworth-Middlesex, from Nikolaus Pevsner, *An Outline of European Architecture,* Baltimore 1960.

179. Friedrich Hewicker, Kaltenkirchen.

180. Courtesy Prestel Verlag, Munich. Photo: Erich Müller.

181. Reproduced by permission of Giulio Einaudi Editore, Turin, from Paolo Portoghesi and Bruno Zevi (editors), *Michelangiolo Architetto,* 1964.

182. Reproduced by permission of Giulio Einaudi Editore, Turin, from Paolo Portoghesi and Bruno Zevi (editors), *Michelangiolo Architetto,* 1964.

183. Alinari-Anderson.

184. Reproduced by permission of Penguin Books Ltd., Harmondsworth-Middlesex, from G. H. Hamilton, *The Art and Architecture of Russia,* Baltimore 1954.

185. Reproduced by permission of Penguin Books Ltd., Harmondsworth-Middlesex, from George Kubler and Martin Soria, *Art and Architecture in Spain and Portugal and Their American Dominions, 1500–1800,* Baltimore 1959.

186. Reproduced by permission of Touring Club Italiano, Milan, from L. V. Bertanelli (editor), *Guida d'Italia, Lazio,* 1935.

187. Reproduced by permission of Alec Tiranti Ltd., London, from J. C. Shepherd and G. A. Jellicoe, *Italian Gardens of the Renaissance,* 1953.

188. Courtesy Louis I. Kahn.

189. Alinari.

190. Reproduced by permission of Rudolf Wittkower, from his book, *Art and Architecture in Italy, 1600–1750,* Penguin Books, Inc., Baltimore 1958.

191. Riccardo Moncalvo, Turin.

192. Heikki Havas, Helsinki.

193. Reproduced by permission of Arkady, Warsaw, from Maria and Kazimierz Piechotka, *Wooden Synagogues,* 1959.

194. Reproduced by permission of George Wittenborn, Inc., New York, from Karl Fleig (editor), *Alvar Aalto,* 1963.

195. G. Kleine-Tebbe, Bremen.

196. From *Architectural Forum,* February 1950.

197. From *Architectural Forum,* February 1950.

198. Reproduced by permission of The University of North Carolina Press, Chapel Hill, from Thomas Tileston Waterman, *The Mansions of Virginia, 1706–1776,* 1946. © 1945.

199. Robert Venturi.

200. Reproduced by permission of Herold Druck- und Verlagsgesellschaft M.B.H., Vienna, from Hans Sedlmayr, *Johann Bernhard Fischer von Erlach,* 1956.

201. Alinari.

202. From *Casabella,* no. 217, 1957.

203. Reproduced by permission of Alec Tiranti Ltd., London, from J. C. Shepherd and G. A. Jellicoe, *Italian Gardens of the Renaissance,* 1953.

204. Touring Club Italiano, Milan.

205. The Museum of Modern Art.

206. Reproduced by permission of Penguin Books Ltd., Harmondsworth-Middlesex, from Nikolaus Pevsner, *An Outline of European Architecture,* Baltimore 1960.

207. Soprintendenza alle Gallerie, Florence.

208. Istituto Centrale del Restauro, Rome.

209. Collection: The Whitney Museum of American Art.

210. Courtesy André Emmerich Gallery.

211. Photo by John Szarkowski, author of *The Idea of Louis Sullivan,* The University of Minnesota Press, Minneapolis. © 1956 The University of Minnesota.

212. Soprintendenza alle Gallerie, Florence.

213. Hirmer Fotoarchiv, Munich.

214. Hirmer Fotoarchiv, Munich.

215. From Colen Campbell, *Vitruvius Britannicus,* vol. I, London 1715.

216. From John Woolfe and James Gandon, *Vitruvius Britannicus,* vol. V, London 1771.

217. Courtesy City Museum and Art Gallery, Birmingham.

218. Robert Venturi.

219. Robert Venturi.

220. Robert Venturi.

221. Robert Venturi.

222. Reproduced by permission of Electa Editrice, Milan, from *Palladio,* 1951.

223. H. Roger-Viollet, Paris.

224. Slide Collection, University of Pennsylvania.

225. From I. T. Frary, *Thomas Jefferson, Architect and Builder,* Garrett and Massie, Inc., Richmond 1939.

226. Robert Venturi.

227. From Colen Campbell *Vitruvius Britannicus,* vols. I and III, London 1715 and 1725.

228. Reproduced by permission of Penguin Books Ltd., Harmondsworth-Middlesex, from Nikolaus Pevsner, *An Outline of European Architecture,* Baltimore 1960.

229. Bildarchiv Foto Marburg, Marburg/Lahn.

230. From Leonardo Benevolo, "Le Chiese Barocche Valsesiane," *Quaderni dell'Istituto di Storia dell'Architettura*, NN. 22–24, Rome 1957.

231. © Country Life.

232. The Museum of Modern Art.

233. Sheila Hicks.

234. Reproduced by permission of Connaissance des Arts, Paris, from Stephanie Faniel, *French Art of the 18th Century*, 1957.

235. Chicago Architectural Photo Co.

236. Bayerische Verwaltung der staatlichen Schlösser, Gärten und Seen, Munich.

237. Courtesy of Anton Schroll and Co., Vienna, from Heinrich Decker, *Romanesque Art in Italy*, 1958.

238. © National Buildings Record, London.

239. Robert Venturi.

240. Reproduced by permission of A. Zwemmer Ltd., London, from Kerry Downes, *Hawksmoor*, 1959.

241. Reproduced by permission of Roberto Pane from his book *Ferdinando Fuga*, Edizioni Scientifiche Italiane, Naples 1961.

242. Italian State Tourist Office.

243. Reproduced by permission of Penguin Books Ltd., Harmondsworth-Middlesex, from Anthony Blunt, *Art and Architecture in France, 1500–1700*, Baltimore 1957.

244. Reproduced by permission of Architectural Book Publishing Co., Inc., New York, from Katharine Hooker and Myron Hunt, *Farmhouses and Small Provincial Buildings in Southern Italy*, 1925.

245. Wayne Andrews.

246. From "Bagnaia," *Quaderni dell'Istituto di Storia dell'Architettura*, N. 17, Rome 1956.

247. Alinari.

248. Reproduced by permission, from *Architectural Design*, December 1962.

249. Reproduced by permission of Architectural Book Publishing Co., Inc., New York, from Katharine Hooker and Myron Hunt, *Farmhouses and Small Provincial Buildings in Southern Italy*, 1925.

250. From Archivo Amigos de Gaudí, Barcelona. Photo: Aleu.

251. Reproduced by permission of George Wittenborn, Inc., New York. from Karl Fleig (editor), *Alvar Aalto*, 1963.

252. George Cserna.

253. Wallace Litwin.

254. Office of Venturi and Rauch.

255. Office of Venturi and Rauch.

256. Office of Venturi and Rauch.

257. Office of Venturi and Rauch.

258. Office of Venturi and Rauch.

259. Office of Venturi and Rauch.

260. Leni Iselin.

261. Leni Iselin.

262. Leni Iselin.

263. Leni Iselin.

264. Edmund B. Gilchrist.

265. Office of Venturi and Rauch.

266. Office of Venturi and Rauch.

267. Office of Venturi and Rauch.

268. Office of Venturi and Rauch.

269. Office of Venturi and Rauch.

270. George Pohl.

271. George Pohl.

272. Office of Venturi and Rauch.

273. George Pohl.

274. George Pohl.

275. George Pohl.

276. George Pohl.

277. Rollin R. La France.

278. Office of Venturi and Rauch.

279. Office of Venturi and Rauch.

280. Office of Venturi and Rauch.

281. Office of Venturi and Rauch.

282. Office of Venturi and Rauch.

283. Office of Venturi and Rauch.

284. Office of Venturi and Rauch.

285. Lawrence S. Williams, Inc.

286. Lawrence S. Williams, Inc.

287. Lawrence S. Williams, Inc.

288. George Pohl.

289. Office of Venturi and Rauch.

290. Office of Venturi and Rauch.

291. Office of Venturi and Rauch.

292. George Pohl.

293. Office of Venturi and Rauch.

294. George Pohl.

295. Office of Venturi and Rauch.

296. Office of Venturi and Rauch.

297. Office of Venturi and Rauch.

298. Office of Venturi and Rauch.

299. Office of Venturi and Rauch.

300. Office of Venturi and Rauch.

301. William Watkins.

302. William Watkins.

303. William Watkins.

304. William Watkins.

305. Office of Venturi and Rauch.

306. Office of Venturi and Rauch.

307. Office of Venturi and Rauch.

308. Rollin R. La France.

309. George Pohl.

310. Rollin R. La France.

311. George Pohl.

312. George Pohl.

313. Rollin R. La France.

314. Rollin R. La France.

315. Rollin R. La France.

316. Rollin R. La France.

317. Office of Venturi and Rauch.

318. Office of Venturi and Rauch.

319. Office of Venturi and Rauch.

320. Rollin R. La France.

321. Rollin R. La France.

322. Rollin R. La France.

323. Office of Venturi and Rauch.

324. Office of Venturi and Rauch.

325. Office of Venturi and Rauch.

326. Office of Venturi and Rauch.

327. Office of Venturi and Rauch.

328. Office of Venturi and Rauch.

329. Office of Venturi and Rauch.

330. George Pohl.

331. George Pohl.

332. Office of Venturi and Rauch.

333. Office of Venturi and Rauch.

334. Office of Venturi and Rauch.

335. Office of Venturi and Rauch.

336. Office of Venturi and Rauch.

337. Office of Venturi and Rauch.

338. Office of Venturi and Rauch.

339. George Pohl.

340. George Pohl.

341. George Pohl.

342. Office of Venturi and Rauch.

343. Office of Venturi and Rauch.

344. Office of Venturi and Rauch.

345. Office of Venturi and Rauch.

346. George Pohl.

347. George Pohl.

348. Office of Venturi and Rauch.

349. Office of Venturi and Rauch.

350. Office of Venturi and Rauch.